# Habitats

# Habitats

Private Lives in the Big City

**CONSTANCE ROSENBLUM**

NEW YORK UNIVERSITY PRESS

*New York and London*

NEW YORK UNIVERSITY PRESS
New York and London
www.nyupress.org

Library of Congress Cataloging-in-Publication Data
Rosenblum, Constance.
Habitats : private lives in the big city / Constance Rosenblum.
pages cm
ISBN 978-0-8147-7154-9 (pb : alk. paper)
ISBN 978-0-8147-7155-6 (e-book)
ISBN 978-0-8147-7156-3 (e-book)
1. Dwellings—New York (State)—New York—History—21st
century. 2. New York (N.Y.)—Social conditions—21st century.
I. Title.
HD7304.N5R59 2013
307.3'36097471—dc23 2012040761

*As always, to Andy and Sarah*

# Contents

# Acknowledgments

**B**ECAUSE all journalistic endeavors are collaborative, there are lots of people to thank.

*The New York Times* was kind enough to allow expanded versions of articles that originally appeared in the paper to be published in book form, along with the accompanying photographs. Alex Ward, the paper's editorial director of book development, was supportive of this project throughout.

At the Real Estate section, my current home at *The Times*, I'm lucky to have the collegiality and friendship of Bill Goss, the section's editor and hands down the nicest person in the world, and my copy editor, Susan Guerrero, who always has my back. Also at *The Times*, I'm grateful to the photographers who created such beautiful images of my subjects and to Phyllis Collazo, who made it so easy to collect the pictures.

When I was struggling to crystallize my thoughts about what it means to have a home in New York City, I got invaluable guidance and inspiration from an assortment of friends and colleagues, among them Manette Berlinger, Akiko Busch, Mark Caldwell, Barbara Cohen, Ellen Hamilton, Susan Hodara, Francis Leadon, Ellen Pall, Wendy Richmond, Beverly Solochek, Lisa Wohl, and Bonnie Yochelson. I'm also grateful to all the friends and colleagues who have suggested so many compelling Habitats subjects over the years; as I constantly reminded them, the column lived on the kindness of other people.

Without my wonderful agent, Andrew Blauner, who supported this project from the beginning, this book would not exist. I'm equally grateful to Eric Zinner at NYU Press and to his terrific colleagues. This is the fourth book I've been lucky enough to do with the Press, and a writer could not ask for a better publisher.

My greatest gratitude is to all my Habitats subjects, both those whose stories are included here and the many others I wish I'd had room to include, and to my husband, Andy, and my daughter, Sarah.

# Introduction

THERE'S an exquisite short story by the writer Laurie Colwin that perfectly captures the lure of living in other people's houses. The story, which is called "The Lone Pilgrim," is about a sensitive and rather lonely young book illustrator whose greatest pleasure is being the ideal houseguest and observing firsthand what she describes as "the closed graceful shapes of other people's lives."

She spends an October night when the moon is full in an old house in a college town, a sleeping dog by the stove, an apple pie in the oven, and atop a window ledge a jar of homemade jam and cuttings of grape ivy in a cracked mug. A rainy night that reminds her of England finds her in a 19th-century brownstone where the mood is set by polished molding, leaded windows, a Spode platter, and a walnut dining table. On yet another occasion, she is ensconced in a house in Maine where the décor includes fancy-back spoons and bouquets of dried flowers in lusterware pitchers.

"The Lone Pilgrim" was published in 1981, a moment when people were becoming increasingly obsessed with the places where they lived, be it lovingly restored town house or reclaimed loft in an abandoned industrial district. But the story speaks to us not simply because Colwin captured a shred of the zeitgeist or because of her lapidary prose. We're also drawn to the subject matter. We're fascinated by what homes and their contents reveal about other people's lives. That's one reason so many people love Victorian novels, with their wealth of domestic detail and their lush evocation of the rooms in which characters' lives unfold. That's why readers are drawn to shelter magazines, with their almost pornographic depictions of lustrous marble and gnarled wood and buttery leather upholstery. It's no accident that people sometimes have dreams about finding secret attics or long-forgotten cellars. They seem to be searching for the perfect home even while asleep.

•

I MYSELF have lived in a few remarkable places, among them the parlor floor of a brownstone straight out of a coming-of-age movie set in Greenwich Village, a prewar building on the Upper West Side at a time when iconic haunts such as the Thalia movie theater and the New Yorker Bookstore still defined the neighborhood, and, for much of my adult life, an apartment in Brooklyn Heights with a spectacular view of the Lower Manhattan skyline and the New York harbor. And for the past few years, I had a chance to follow in the footsteps of Colwin's heroine, sort of, by way of a column called Habitats that appeared regularly in the Real Estate section of *The New York Times*.

Habitats, which was published every week or so and focused on the residents of an individual house or apartment, was a fixture of the Real Estate section from the early 1990s until late 2012. The column endured even in a rapidly changing media environment, I suspect, because readers of *The Times* yearned not only to master the complexities of fixed-rate mortgages and to learn how to outwit finicky co-op boards. They also had an intense desire to look behind other people's front doors and peer into their lives.

In the column's original form, Habitats drew its subject matter from throughout the New York metropolitan area and concentrated largely on matters of design and décor. I'm as much of a sucker as the next person for crown moldings and wide-plank floors. But when I took over the column in the spring of 2009, I realized that I could use this franchise of precious journalistic real estate for a different purpose.

I wanted to use the column to tell more intimate stories. I wanted to use the physical nature of a home as a wedge to delve into personal history, and to produce, as one reader nicely put it, biography through real estate. I loved that phrase because it struck me as a wonderfully apt description of exactly what I was trying to do. The lives of the people who inhabited these places were easily as absorbing as the homes themselves, often far more so, and the intersection between person and place was endlessly provocative, endlessly engaging.

I had other goals. As is evident from the 40 columns in this collection, expanded versions of pieces that were originally published in the newspaper, I wanted the columns to range as widely as possible in terms of the subjects' ages, ethnic backgrounds, professions, family structure, and socioeconomic status. At the same time, I wanted to focus on people who lived within the five boroughs.

It's hard to imagine richer and more varied subject matter than the places New Yorkers call home. There may be eight million stories in the Naked City, as the tagline to the old TV show puts it. But there are also nearly three million dwelling places, ranging from Park Avenue palaces to Dickensian garrets and encompassing much in between. The physical details of these residences—the décor, the keepsakes, the money spent, the junk amassed—are invariably fascinating. In a city so rich in architectural history and variety of family type, ethnic background, economic status, and personal taste, what you find when you walk through someone else's front door can't help but be intriguing.

And taken as a whole, the columns also offer a mosaic of domestic life in one of the great cities of the world. They open windows onto forgotten corners of a huge metropolis—the beachfront cottage at the end of the subway line, the dingy apartment in a public housing tower, the basement studio invisible from the street. They introduce us to neighborhoods so exotic they might be on the other side of the globe. They bear witness to the justly famed variety of New York architecture—converted tenements, co-ops born of the political passion of an earlier era, gracious brownstones, jaw-dropping mansions. They remind us that economic inequality defines New York as it defines few other places.

The stories of the largely unknown New Yorkers who inhabit these homes are compelling. What are their dreams, their fears, their obsessions, their secrets? What does the place where they live reveal about who they really are and who they long to be? And there's an even more provocative question to be asked: What makes a home in New York distinctive, even singular? Expressed another way, what do New York's houses and apartments have in common with one another, despite their varied faces? What can be said about these homes that can't be said of the homes of Bostonians or Vermonters or the suburbanites of Westchester County?

The answers are elusive.

Despite all that has been written about the city in the four centuries since the first Europeans set foot on what came to be known as New York, and despite the exploding number of works exploring the nature of domestic life and its impact on our souls and our psyches, the literature on the intersection of these two subjects is unexpectedly thin. Much of what we know we've learned from novelists such as Edith Wharton, whose depictions of Gilded Age New York echo in our minds every time we walk down certain gracious, tree-lined streets, or from historians such as Robert Caro, whose horrific descriptions of the slums of the South Bronx in his biography of Robert Moses are nearly as terrifying as the real thing.

There are also a handful of classic essays that help define what it means to be a New Yorker and how people make a place for themselves in this most rewarding and challenging of settings. One of the most memorable of these essays is F. Scott Fitzgerald's "My Lost City," a work that captures the texture of New York life at two pivotal points in its history. In 1919, Fitzgerald wrote, that shining moment just after the First World War, "New York had all the iridescence of the beginning of the world," and the city seemed "wrapped cool in its mystery and promise." A dozen years later, he bitterly concluded that New York "no longer whispers of fantastic success and eternal youth," that "all is lost save memory." Like generations before him, Fitzgerald had come to New York to invent himself, to realize passionately held dreams and ambitions, but the city that once seemed a place of miracles had turned to dust.

In the celebrated essay "Goodbye to All That," Joan Didion charted the trajectory of a similarly doomed love affair. When Didion moved to New York in the mid-'50s at the age of 20, she, like Fitzgerald, fell passionately in love with her adopted home. "New York was no mere city," Didion wrote of her heady first impressions. "It was instead an infinitely romantic notion, the mysterious nexus of all love and money and power, the shining and perishable dream itself." Eight years later, her ardor had cooled. "I talk about how difficult it would be for us to 'afford' to live in New York right now," she said of her decision to return with her husband to California, "about how much 'space' we would need. All I mean is that I was very young in New York, and that at some point the golden rhythm was broken, and I am not that young anymore."

In "Moving On," published in 2006 in *The New Yorker*, Nora Ephron traced the contours of an even more site-specific urban romance. The object of her affection was her five-bedroom apartment in the Apthorp, the Renaissance Revival palace on West 78th Street. Badly bruised after a divorce, Ephron had moved to the Apthorp in 1980, and for more than two decades, her besottedness with her apartment knew no bounds. "I was planning to live there forever," she wrote. "Til death did us part." But her rent soared, her building shed its raffish charm, and she eventually decamped across town. Although her new place proved perfectly satisfactory, something was lost. "I am never going to dream about this new apartment of mine," Ephron concluded. "It's not love. It's just where I live."

These essays tell us a great deal about the glory and heartbreak that can await those who seek a foothold in this particular place. But the most enduring statement of what it means to be a New Yorker isn't an account of a doomed affair or a story of dashed dreams. It's E. B. White's "Here Is New York," an unabashed love letter to the city that was published in 1948 and is studded with observations about life in this city that people have been quoting for more than 60 years.

White made the buoyant pronouncement that "no one should come to New York to live unless he is willing to be lucky." He differentiated among the three kinds of New Yorkers—the natives, the commuters, and the settlers from elsewhere who came here in quest of something and who in his opinion are the ones who give the city its passion. Writing at the dawn of the nuclear age, White offered eerie intimations of the attacks of September 11, reminding us that "a single flight of planes no bigger than a wedge of geese can quickly end this island fantasy, burn the towers, . . . cremate the millions." And he provided one of the most poignant descriptions of the bounties New York can bestow: "The gift of privacy, the jewel of loneliness."

•

THAT White singled out loneliness and privacy as the signature benefits of a metropolis defined by density and density's urban twin, verticality, isn't surprising. Despite the congestion, it's easy to find privacy in the city, which is why hidden realms flourish behind the city's closed doors, whether it be immigrant cultures imported from half a world away or lives lived nearly off the grid even as the city thrums with ever more cutting-edge technology. Despite the fact that solitude can seem an elusive gift, there's also truth to the cliché: it's easy to feel alone in a crowd. During my journeys around the city, I sometimes sensed a loneliness, especially among women, no longer young, who lived by themselves. I sometimes thought of Wharton's Lily Bart, friendless and ultimately doomed in her small, cheerless room with the flowerpot on the window ledge.

Lily Bart passed the last chapter of her life in a boarding house, but I remembered her final dwelling place as an apartment, perhaps because there's no more defining expression of life in this tall and congested metropolis. The city is home to more than two million apartments, located not just in slender Manhattan but also in the boroughs beyond, and in their size and configuration, they're as much an icon of New York as the skyline and Times Square. The New York apartment is the perch from which Holly Golightly and the intrepid sisters of *Wonderful Town* set out to storm the city. The New York apartment—that is to say, a rental, not a pricy co-op—is the quintessential emblem of young life, the place where you live when you're poor, footloose, adventurous, and more in love with the city than you'll ever be again.

These apartments have a porous quality. Walking down a brownstone-lined street at twilight, it's impossible not to peer into one after another lighted window and marvel at the winking chandeliers, the glossy shutters, the well-stocked bookshelves. It's thanks to the voyeur in all of us that the film *Rear Window* has become the definitive statement about the sometimes oddly public nature of apartment life in New York. The skin separating inside and outside shifts and flutters like a theatrical scrim—one moment transparent, the next opaque.

The city's apartments by their very nature are also apt to be small, so small that people who have an unusually large space apologize for all the rooms. Except for the extremely wealthy or the extremely lucky, chances are good that New Yorkers live in a shoebox, which is why we know the square footage of our place down to the last inch. As housing in New York grows ever costlier, some places seem so tiny as to be uninhabitable. This is especially true for people in the arts, for whom low-cost housing, no matter how confining, can mean the difference between pursuing a career in the city and slinking back home, tail between legs, to Wichita or Syracuse or Dubuque. And given all those little apartments packed tightly together, the need for temporary escape can be overwhelming, which is why New Yorkers lucky enough to have country houses consider themselves blessed beyond words.

At the same time, these little spaces frequently explode with creativity; rare is the apartment furnished entirely by way of Kmart or even Ikea, much as New Yorkers love those emporiums. Even well-heeled New Yorkers aren't ashamed to rummage around the street (although less in the age of bedbugs) or the local Housing Works. Because everything is so compressed, the total effect is often dazzling.

All these apartments arranged like upended egg cartons guarantee that New Yorkers share a few other things. One has to do with the primacy of views, especially prized because your nearest neighbor likely lives just inches from the tip of your nose. If you have a view, you probably brag about it ad nauseam. If you don't, maybe you have something to compensate, like a nice wood-burning fireplace.

New Yorkers are also defined by the number of stairs we climb to get to our apartments or, for the luckier among us, by the elevator. It's understandable that middle-class families in Brooklyn and the Bronx felt that they had arrived when they moved from a dreary walk-up to a new elevator building or, for a later generation, to that "deluxe apartment in the sky." Understandably also, a New Yorker's greatest fear is to be trapped in a stalled elevator. The story of the Chinese restaurant delivery man stranded for 81 hours in an elevator in a 38-story apartment house in the Bronx struck terror in many hearts; that could have been us.

Except, perhaps, in the far reaches of bucolic Staten Island, New Yorkers are also defined by the closeness of neighbors. We hear the Clementi piano exercises from across the hall, the kid upstairs endlessly bouncing a ball, the lovers' quarrel, the slammed doors, the weeping—it's hardly a surprise that New Yorkers are obsessed with acoustical privacy. Nor are these intrusions necessarily comforting. We smell the aroma of unfamiliar ingredients wafting down the hall; we hear languages we can't identify in the lobby. But ideally, our closeness to one another teaches lessons of tolerance and kindness, especially in a city with such diversity, home to a record number of immigrants who maintain increasingly close ties to their homelands and are under ever less pressure to assimilate. This closeness also leads to shared memories of defining events—blackouts, doormen strikes, garbage strikes, and now trumping everything else, the attacks of September 11.

New Yorkers are defined, too, by the primacy of the subway, a system that binds even city residents who live miles from the nearest stop. And only here would people still be debating the candy-colored loops and swirls of a subway map designed four decades ago.

The novelist Jonathan Lethem once described New York as a city of "stairwells and elevator shafts," a place of "claustrophobic compression." That pretty much sums it up. It's understandable that claustrophobics, terrified of elevators and other small spaces, have such a hard time here. (Acrophobics, with their fear of heights, don't do so well either.) But as White observed 60-odd years ago, "New Yorkers do not crave comfort and convenience. If they did, they would live elsewhere."

•

ONE reason we New Yorkers can tolerate all this congestion and compression is because our homes embrace so much of the world beyond our doors. The entire city is our front yard, our back yard, our living room, our play room. New Yorkers cram themselves into tiny apartments and endure cheek-by-jowl domestic arrangements knowing that just a few steps away is magnificent Central Park or Prospect Park or, for Brooklyn

Heights residents, the Promenade, which reminds me of some glamorous European boulevard every time I set foot on its newly restored paving blocks. Or your second home is the playground, especially at a certain stage of life. "Remember how we lived at the playground?" a mother friend from the neighborhood asked wistfully of the days when our children were young and our entire lives seemed to unfold within sight of swings and sandboxes.

The stoop, the street, even the vest-pocket park, no matter how small and scraggly—all are part of what New Yorkers talk about when they talk about home. That sentiment helps explain why New Yorkers are obsessed by their neighborhoods, right down to the sometimes cloyingly clever names (BoCoCa? BelDel?). In this city, your neighborhood is as much your home as your walk-up or your studio or your floor-through.

Jane Jacobs understood the central role of New York's public spaces better than most; her portrait of her block of Hudson Street in Greenwich Village, with its buzzy street life and assortment of shops—the butcher, the locksmith, the fruit stand, the deli—is the best-remembered part of *The Death and Life of Great American Cities*, her classic study of urban life. Jacobs grasped what makes a city simultaneously vital and nurturing. And even though New York has been transformed in the half century since her book was published, despite the invasion of Duane Reades and bank branches and cell phone stores, hers is a classic description of what New Yorkers picture, or would like to picture, when they think about the street where they live.

There's a reason that the High Line, the landscaped park built atop a historic rail line on Manhattan's West Side, holds such a soft spot in the hearts of New Yorkers. It's not because of its size—even when completed, the strip will extend only a mile and a half. We love this quirky new urban space because the High Line by its mere existence adds a wonderfully original room to every house and apartment in the city.

•

IF New York is a city in which your home extends well beyond your front door, it's also a place where a disproportionately large number of people live in places that are very old. Census data show that 85 percent of New Yorkers live in buildings erected before 1970, compared with 42 percent of Americans generally. Even more remarkably, 39 percent of New Yorkers live in buildings constructed before 1930 and 17 percent in buildings predating 1920.

Thanks to the venerable nature of New York's housing stock, entire neighborhoods function as palimpsests of the city's history. All those 19th-century brownstones and row houses and turn-of-the-century industrial lofts and prewar apartment houses speak so eloquently to fabled eras in the city's history that even the most up-to-the-minute New Yorkers feel as if they live among ghosts. The past hangs heavy upon us. Neighborhoods, streets, even individual buildings are saturated with memory, serving as mute reminders of those who occupied these spaces long before we did. Their history becomes ours.

These ghosts take different forms. Many of my Habitats subjects were aware of living on the footprint of the place where their own ancestors had lived or where they themselves had lived for decades. They were conscious of living in neighborhoods with long and storied histories, such as SoHo and the brownstone districts of Manhattan and Brooklyn, or in buildings such as the bungalows of Rockaway, evocative reminders of how working-class New Yorkers passed their summers generations earlier.

Perhaps because so many New Yorkers live atop past lives, we're also united by nostalgia for the city that was. "No matter how long you have been here, you are a New Yorker the first time you say, That used to be Munsey's, or That used to be the Tic Toc Lounge," Colson Whitehead wrote shortly after the attacks of September 11, a moment when people were struggling to articulate their feelings about the city that had been struck such a devastating blow. "That before the internet café plugged itself in, you got your shoes resoled in the mom-and-pop operation that used to be there. You are a New Yorker when what was there before is more real and solid than what is here now."

Even the hipster, arrived in Brooklyn minutes ago, has been known to complain, "I miss the old Brooklyn" as one more designer stroller edges into one more ultracool brunch spot in Williamsburg, a neighborhood that the writer Robert Anasi mournfully christened "the last Bohemia." In few other cities is the longing for the golden age just beyond our reach so potent.

As neighborhoods morph before our eyes—first SoHo, then the Lower East Side, then the great swath of Brooklyn neighborhoods strung along the L line, then who knows what next—we ache for what we've lost. Perhaps this longing helps explain the photographs of long-departed ancestors that decorate the houses and apartments of so many of the New Yorkers I interviewed. Sometimes the ancestors aren't even their own but rather evocations of a communal past, as if the city's bureaus and night tables and living room walls functioned like the totem poles of the Northwest Coast Indians, carved with beavers and ravens and whales that represent various faces of a shared history.

•

JUST as the history of New York's streets and buildings and neighborhoods becomes our history, so are our feelings about where we live defined by cultural artifacts that have taken the city as their subject matter. Consciously or not, when New Yorkers talk about home, we're often talking about a scene from a movie or a lyric from a song. These words and images teach us how to be New Yorkers and, as surely as all those apps and guidebooks, show us what sorts of lives are possible here—bohemian catch-as-catch-can lives on the once-scruffy Lower East Side, lives of liberal respectability in the apartment houses of the Upper West Side, cozy domesticity in the brownstones of Park Slope, moneyed elegance in the town houses of the Upper East Side. They tell us how others have lived here in the past and how we ourselves might live. In these creations, we find templates for our own existences.

New York is hardly unique in having inspired a cultural outpouring of such scope. Even people who have never set foot in London or Paris or San Francisco feel as if they know these cities intimately, thanks to books they've read, movies they've watched, songs they've listened to. But to name all the works of art inspired by New York would be a nearly impossible task.

And so we see the city through artists' eyes. Walking down certain streets, New Yorkers of a certain generation invariably remember Wharton's observation about buildings that look as if they've been coated with cold chocolate sauce. They circle Washington Square with the friendly companionship of Henry James. They see the hand of Edward Hopper in every water tower, the hand of Alfred Stieglitz or Edward Steichen in the image of the Flatiron Building on a rainy night. In their mind, they hear the mournful strains of Simon and Garfunkel while waiting for a train in a grimy subway station.

We learn of New York's giddiness from Fitzgerald and from such novels as *Bright Lights, Big City.* We learn of its loneliness from the Delmore Schwartz story "In Dreams Begin Responsibilities" and its surliness from Richard Prince. We learn of its exuberance through the musical *On the Town*, its misery through *Rent*. Sometimes the work of art seems more authentic than the real thing. Above my living room sofa hangs an engraving of the Brooklyn waterfront in winter, circa 1820, showing tiny bundled-up figures set against small clapboard houses. When I picture my neighborhood, this is the image in my mind's eye.

Music captures what it means to be a New Yorker in almost hallucinatory fashion, especially the romance of Manhattan at a certain giddy moment in the city's history. Wilfrid Sheed, in his book *The House That George Built*, explains why so much of the American songbook has shaped our perceptions of what it means to live in New York and to be a New Yorker. Except for Cole Porter, Sheed reminds us, "all the first generation of the Jazz Age were city guys writing primarily for city people"—and not just city guys but New York guys: Izzy Baline from the Lower East Side, who became Irving Berlin of the Upper East Side, and especially George Gershwin, that quintessential Upper West Sider and unrivaled interpreter of the soundscape that is New York. "Gershwin captured the screaming clangor of New York," Sheed reminds us. "Gershwin was Times Square at night, and skyscrapers and jackhammers by day."

If music provides the soundtrack for the life a New Yorker might lead, movies furnish the pictures and have ever since the dawn of the art form. In large part, the city has been defined for us by flickering images on a screen; as James Sanders writes in *Celluloid Skyline: New York and the Movies*, "Alongside the real city in which we live, there exists a mythic New York, a dream city, brought to life in thousands of feature films, which for generations has captured the imagination of people all around the world." People from elsewhere frequently confess that this "movie city" played a significant role in bringing them to New York, and on some level, they believe that this dream city will be waiting for them once they arrive. They expect to see Fred and Ginger dancing across the rooftops.

In enumerating the movies that have shaped our impression of the city, the temptation is to simply tick off title after title. From the years before and after the Second World War: *The Thin Man*, *Marty*, *Sweet Smell of Success*, and *On the Waterfront*. From the '60s: *Midnight Cowboy*, *Rosemary's Baby* (with its brooding images of the Dakota), and of course *Breakfast at Tiffany's*. From the '70s, the decade that produced some of the greatest movie portraits of the city: *Klute*, *Carnal Knowledge*, *Death Wish*, *Harry and Tonto*, *The Taking of Pelham 123*, *Saturday Night Fever*, *An Unmarried Woman* (costarring a spectacular Upper East Side apartment coveted by many members of the audience), *The French Connection*, *The Wanderers*, and *Next Stop, Greenwich Village*. From the

'80s and '90s: *Sophie's Choice, Tootsie, Ghostbusters, Desperately Seeking Susan, Wall Street, Crossing Delancey,* and *Working Girl.*

And of course there's Woody Allen's trio of rhapsodic valentines to the city—*Manhattan, Annie Hall,* and *Hannah and Her Sisters*—along with everything by Spike Lee, nearly everything by Sidney Lumet and Martin Scorsese, and a few memorable cinematic portraits by Nora Ephron. Brooklyn has inspired a whole subset of films, among them *Moonstruck,* adored even though it plays fast and loose with the borough's geography, and *The Squid and the Whale,* the definitive portrait of the early days of gentrification in Park Slope. And an entire generation has been schooled as to what it's like to be a New Yorker, thanks to TV series such as *Seinfeld* and 20 years of television's *Law & Order,* not to mention reruns likely to continue into the next millennium.

Along with instructing us on how to be New Yorkers, this cultural outpouring nourishes our sense that we live in a place of importance. E. B. White reminds us that New Yorkers share "the sense of belonging to something unique, cosmopolitan, mighty and unparalleled," and to a great extent these cultural artifacts reinforce the feeling that we live in a singular, world-class city. When Frank Sinatra sings those rousing words, "If I can make it there, I'll make it anywhere," he touches a nerve because he reminds us how proud we can be to live in this maddening, challenging place. So does the rapper Jay-Z, who updated those sentiments for a new generation: "Yeah, I'm out that Brooklyn, now I'm down in TriBeCa, right next to DeNiro, but I'll be 'hood forever, I'm the new Sinatra, and . . . since I made it here, I can make it anywhere." Jay-Z's words are cooler, but the sentiment remains the same.

•

NORA EPHRON confessed that she had dreams about her old apartment. For a great many New Yorkers, however, such dreams take the shape of nightmares. Despite the sheen, New York is an ever more formidable place. In terms of money, space, and the pace of urban life, the city is daunting on many levels. The real estate maze presents a legendary obstacle course, or as Jack Donaghy summed up the situation in the TV series *30 Rock,* "In Manhattan real estate, there are no rules; it's like check-in at an Italian airport." If you're young and starting out in New York, few things are more stressful than finding a place to live. As prices soar, a task that was never easy has become apocalyptically difficult.

And while the rewards are great, among them the chance to escape a stifling small town or to establish an apartment out from under the parental thumb or to live among like-minded peers in a neighborhood vibrant with youth and creativity, these rewards are hard won. As the gap between rich and poor grows cavernous, as the middle class shrinks, the financial grid that governs life in the metropolis offers little give, especially for people just beginning their lives here.

For newcomers, the challenges are especially arduous. When they arrive, they must make radical adjustments on every front—space, costs, logistics, and much else. Typically they move again and again, seeking something better, escaping something awful. The competition—for the apartment, the job, the boyfriend, the perfect shoes—can overwhelm. The fear of missing out—the dreaded FOMO—can prove paralyzing. The city's nonstop contentiousness can rub raw the most resilient New Yorker. It's hardly surprising that even ardent New Yorkers have a complicated love-hate relationship with the city, complaining endlessly about the rents, the subway, the cops, the mayor, the traffic, the crowds, you name it, even while insisting that they wouldn't leave for the world.

Some people adapt gracefully and creatively. Others tell horror stories. When Sinatra sings that anthem, he's acknowledging New Yorkers' pride of place but also offering a tip of the hat to the challenges they face in creating a life for themselves here.

And so when you return to the place where you live, the relief is palpable. I remember thinking this on the night of a terrible storm when my daughter, wet and bedraggled at the end of a long day in Manhattan, finally made her way back to Brooklyn. "All I wanted was to get home," she announced as she straggled in, soaked but triumphant. And I was glad she had made it.

# Starting Out

# 1

# His Hacienda in the Sky

### Boris Fishman on the Lower East Side

JUNE 21, 2009

Boris Fishman, a Russian-born writer, in his Mexican-themed aerie on the Lower East Side. (Ruby Washington/*The New York Times*)

I N 2003, with the most loving intentions, a Russian immigrant couple named Yakov Fishman and Anna Oder helped their only child buy a $180,000 studio apartment on the Upper East Side.

The father, a skilled craftsman possessed of what his son, Boris Fishman, then 24, described as "hands of gold," insisted on painting the walls gray, beige, and off-white—meek colors reflecting roots in a country where risk-taking could be perilous, especially for Jewish families such as this one. The setting that resulted was irreproachably tasteful and serious and, in the eyes of its occupant, as confining as a coffin, albeit one that could have leaped out of the pages of *Architectural Digest*. "It was very comforting, but I wasn't ready for comfort," says Mr. Fishman, a freelance writer whose broad forehead and dark features bespeak his Slavic heritage. "I was looking for my own identity. I wanted something more rough-edged, a place where I could throw bold colors onto the wall and didn't have to walk carefully.

"I wanted to respect what my parents had done," he is careful to add, aware of how arduous it can be to establish one's independence, especially when the quest pits immigrant parents shaped by tradition against an increasingly Americanized child. "But at the end of the day, it was their place as much as mine."

Today, Mr. Fishman lives 15 stories above the remnants of the old Lower East Side, in a one-bedroom aerie ablaze with the warmth and decorative touches of a Mexican village. The colors of the walls are so intense, you almost feel heat rising from them. What he affectionately describes as his "hacienda in the sky" has the delightful randomness of a Victorian cabinet of wonders, its ingredients assembled from sources as disparate as indigenous craftspeople half a world away and the big-box store down the street.

Mr. Fishman's journey to this setting reveals a great deal about coming of age, finding one's identity apart from one's parents, and a search for a sense of home thousands of miles from one's true homeland. But before embarking on this quest, he first had to attack a space best described as a dump.

The building, on Grand Street near the F.D.R. Drive, is part of East River Houses, a cluster of red-brick towers constructed in the mid-1950s as moderate-income co-ops. It seems fitting that this idealistic son of Russia ended up in a complex whose original mission was to offer a piece of the American dream to thousands of postwar, middle-income families and whose early days were wreathed with optimism and a sense of promise. The project's beguiling logo—diminutive twin pine trees standing arm in arm—still adorns a sign outside Mr. Fishman's building.

The tenant who had occupied the apartment that Mr. Fishman bought for about $400,000 had been there pretty much since East River Houses opened and had left behind for posterity a bathtub turned orange from rust, carpeting choked with dust, and a pair of dentures that sat uncovered in a plastic container in the medicine cabinet. "It was kind of terrifying," Mr. Fishman says of the scene that greeted him when he arrived in the fall of 2005.

Unsurprisingly, given that the Soviet Union disintegrated just three years after his family fled its constraints and headed to America, Mr. Fishman is obsessed with exploring the roots of his Russianness. As he asked in an essay exploring his ambivalent relationship with his homeland, "What does it mean to be from a place that no longer exists on the map?" Yet inspiration for ways to make these sad rooms his own came from a very different source—visits to Mexican cities like Oaxaca and Xalapa, favorite vacation destinations for this child of bone-chilling Russian winters. His first night in Oaxaca provided a seminal moment.

"I was standing in the central plaza, listening to the bells from the cathedral," Mr. Fishman recalls of the scene. "Shops were open; teenagers were hanging around, flirting; families were strolling about. The idea of evenings devoted to leisure and conversation, brass bands playing spontaneously, women dancing on the cobblestone streets—I felt connected to the scene because it felt so European."

Paradoxically, the warmth and sense of community reminded him of Minsk, the city in Belarus where he had spent his childhood. Six months and $15,000 later, he had produced a series of spaces that captured the look and especially the vitality of semitropical Mexico, albeit within the unlikely setting of a drab high-rise.

The apartment's showstopper, drawn with a felt-tipped marker on a living room wall, is a menu from a favorite restaurant in Xalapa, featuring such items as "enchiladas de la casa (4) MX $47" and "tostadas de pollo (3) MX $42." (Like the responsible journalist he is, Mr. Fishman credits his source: "With appreciation to Hosteria la Candela, Xalapa, Veracruz, Mexico.") To the right hang black-and-white photographs of Guatemalan refugees in Mexico, reminiscent of displays found in the hipper restaurants in Mexican university towns, where work by a local artist invariably hangs on the wall next to the menu. Atop these arrange-

19

ments, the words "casa de los trotamundos" are emblazoned on lustrous orange tiles. "House of the world-trotters," Mr. Fishman translates. "I know. It's corny."

The unrenovated kitchen features a friendly mishmash of original '50s fixtures, including what Mr. Fishman describes as an awesome porcelain sink. On one wall, a checkerboard of yellow, orange, red, and green tiles suggests an abstracted New York skyline, a tip of the hat to Mr. Fishman's evolving love affair with the city to which he was transplanted in 1988, a 9-year-old with a funny haircut. The bedroom is relatively spare, but its windows, like those in the living room, face west and north onto one of those views beloved by hard-core New Yorkers—a forest of high-rises framed by the Manhattan and Williamsburg Bridges. The sunsets, needless to say, are spectacular.

Each room is painted a different saturated color—the living room is rust, the kitchen rose, the bathroom Mediterranean sky, the bedroom a medley of greens. Dangling over doorways and peeking out of alcoves are folkish little items that manage the neat trick of being beguiling without sinking into kitsch. Dollhouse-sized chairs from Mexico with matchbox seats are affixed to walls. Décor includes an emerald plate from Morocco, a faux old-gold mirror and embossed slabs of electric-blue tin. A tin pressing honors "Our Mother: St. John of the Lakes."

And as much as Mr. Fishman sought to shake off parental influences in his new place, his father's spirit is palpable. But this time around, the influence is deeply satisfying.

The elder Mr. Fishman, now a doorman in a building on the Upper East Side, was a house painter back home—Russian Jews needed modest career goals—and early on he took steps to ensure that his son would never have the option of resorting to manual work. The son remembers the image of his father atop a stepladder in the family's apartment, the air redolent with the smells of paint and varnish, his father's small, beautiful hands perpetually chapped.

"What are you doing?" the curious child would ask.

"Go study," the father would reply.

"He refused to teach me his skills," Mr. Fishman explains, and at the time he passionately resented his father's stance. But the years have transformed and softened their relationship, and this apartment is filled with evidence of his father's virtuosity, including a rough-hewn reading bench made of thickly varnished painted pine and fitted with iron hardware, along with a desk at which Mr. Fishman writes every day. Both men helped fashion these pieces, and as the two worked side by side, the son finally learned from the father, as he had yearned to do. This dynamic is a subject Mr. Fishman explores in a book he's writing about masculinity, tentatively titled "An American Son."

Today, the apartment looks as if all the elements came together effortlessly. Dream on, says Mr. Fishman, who can reel off mistake after mistake, among them walls that had to be repainted again and again because the colors were too intense. He had to unscrew the front door because, as a decorating rookie, he never thought to measure the dining room table he bought from a Housing Works thrift shop. And don't get him started on the traumas involving the lamp shades in the bedroom.

During the months Mr. Fishman was knee-deep in wood samples and paint chips, he was also negotiating the shoals of a complicated personal relationship. Eventually, his obsession with hardware catalogues and to-do lists made maintaining that relationship untenable, and he's the first to admit that he couldn't have been easy to live with during that period. "At one point, I must have had 15 tile catalogues and endless notebooks," he confesses. "Really, I was a miserable wretch."

But the apartment became a companion of sorts, the setting for a dozen housewarmings, along with parties for friends. And on a recent evening, as Mr. Fishman sat shoeless in the living room, gazing at the pinpoint lights outlining the bridges and the glittering traffic that raced across them, he seemed to be a character in one of those period films about the glamour of the big city. Plus the renovation taught him a few things. "The whole undertaking was terrifying," Mr. Fishman says, "partly because I came from an environment where all risk was to be avoided. And of course mistakes were never part of the process uptown. But I have learned to make peace with my mistakes."

# 2

# A Single Man Buys a Home for Someday

## Steve Chung in Carroll Gardens, Brooklyn

**JULY 4, 2010**

Steve Chung, a 37-year-old lawyer, in a converted doll factory in Carroll Gardens, Brooklyn. (Brian Harkin for *The New York Times*)

I N 2006, when Steve Chung began shopping for a new apartment, he wasn't seeking what you might expect from a single, 30-something lawyer ensconced in the heart of the East Village. At the time, Mr. Chung was living in a one-bedroom opposite the Beauty Bar, a boisterous hipster outpost on East 14th Street, and he had neither wife nor child, nor even a serious girlfriend. Nevertheless, his goal was finding a place that was in a family-friendly neighborhood and was large enough to accommodate a wife and children.

"When I was looking, prices were skyrocketing, and I feared there was no end in sight," says Mr. Chung, who is 37 and works as a media lawyer for NBC Universal specializing in First Amendment issues. "Plus, I'm a little crazy when it comes to planning in advance. So even though I was single, and with no serious prospects and no kids, I wanted to buy an apartment that was located in a good school district and had room for a small family."

Carroll Gardens in Brooklyn seemed promising. "I walked around this area, and I saw that a Whole Foods was opening up and figured there was a lot of potential," he says. As industriously as any parent of a toddler, he checked out local schools. In 2007, after visiting dozens of places, Mr. Chung settled on a $650,000 condominium on Smith Street in an old industrial building that had done time as a dairy store and a doll factory. The apartment had three bedrooms and was just a block from Public School 58, considered one of the city's best. And while Whole Foods never arrived and longstanding pollution problems led to designation of nearby Gowanus Canal as a Superfund site, Mr. Chung doesn't regret his decision.

The family that he anticipated hasn't yet come along, or as he sums up the situation, "My whole plan to acquire a place to start a family was a good one, except that I have no family. That was the only flaw." On the plus side, he now possesses a whimsical duplex, a glittery concoction of colored glass bricks, animal motifs run riot, and unexpected architectural touches executed with a palette straight out of a child's box of crayons.

When Mr. Chung moved into the apartment, he found himself confronted with a look that he came to call "French farmhouse," one that featured an all-white décor heavy on wooden beams, exposed brick, and arched doorways and interior windows wreathed in swags of red velvet. The previous owner had used the space as a music studio, and furnishings included giant slabs of marble, Persian rugs, oversized mirrors, and a grand piano. "It definitely had a point of view," Mr. Chung says. "It just wasn't my point of view."

Not that he wanted something bland. His goal was to avoid what he describes as "the typical law-firm décor," a style he found dark and even oppressive. "I remember walking into the office of a large law firm," he says, "and feeling as if the walls were closing in on me, with all the stoic woods and bank-colored greens."

As Mr. Chung was pondering these matters, he came across a magazine article about designers who help New Yorkers remake their apartments. One firm described itself as a company that served "even people who had no budget," as Mr. Chung remembers it. "So I called them," he says, "and as it turned out, their definition of no budget was $150,000."

He had $5,000. But a member of the firm was kind enough to refer him to a Carroll Gardens designer named Robert Farrell, and Mr. Chung has Mr. Farrell to thank for the look that resulted. "He came to my apartment, made a drawing of the space, and then did a paint-by-numbers type of thing saying which walls should be what colors," Mr. Chung says. "He used little paint chips to indicate exactly what colors he had in mind." The cost for this service: $1,000.

To enter Mr. Chung's apartment today is like gazing at a glowing sunset; you almost have to close your eyes lest the dazzle make you woozy. Walls are saturated reds and yellows. Red, yellow, and blue Panton chairs surround a round wooden picnic table, a thrift-shop find that Mr. Chung painted sky blue. Cherry-wood floors wind through the apartment, as do green, violet, yellow, and clear Italian glass bricks, a happy inheritance from the previous owner. These translucent blocks form skylights on the first level, while upstairs they form part of the floor, giving visitors the disconcerting sense that they're walking on panes of glass.

Mr. Chung has no pets, but given the preponderance of animal motifs, they're hardly missed. A stuffed penguin and a stuffed ape perch on little red schoolroom chairs. A leopard set against a pink background gazes out from a hanging made of balsa wood. A hand-stitched quilt from India that's embroidered with elephants presides over the sofa. Metallic wallpaper with black and silvery swirls that suggest leopard skin covers one wall of the den. A chandelier made of fake antlers hangs from the ceiling, and a small stuffed wolf sits on a rocker whose arms are carved with images of geese. It's a wonder Mr. Chung doesn't have nightmares about being trapped in a zoo.

Another theme is the work of the American outsider artist Henry Darger, a darling of the genre and a favorite of Mr. Chung's. Darger was noted for his quirky aesthetic and his fetching if slightly unsettling images of young girls of an earlier era, and one of Mr. Chung's treasured possessions is a poster featuring a smiling child wearing an old-fashioned dress and a demure bob, an advertisement for the documentary about the artist and his work.

Darger would probably have nice things to say about the contents of the black metal shelves that showcase what Mr. Chung describes as "all the weird things I've collected over the years." The trove includes miniature Japanese robots, a Hawaiian tiki statue, Russian nesting dolls, a sculpture made from a pair of pliers, a plastic toothpick dispenser from Taiwan, a Fisher-Price fire engine that was Mr. Chung's when he was 4, and a small box with gold lettering from Ladurée, the Paris patisserie. There are also five ukuleles, including one made from a cigar box that's dated 1886 and bears the label "Sam'l Davis, the Vintage Cigar."

Mr. Chung has not yet acquired the family he hoped for. And some people might question the wisdom of creating such a deeply personal environment, right down to the last violet glass brick and stuffed penguin. Where in this setting would there be room for someone with her own aesthetic? What if a future wife didn't care to live among Darger's little girls or have a taste for wallpaper that resembled leopard skin?

The apartment's owner acknowledges that not everyone shares his taste. "I love my apartment because it has a sense of fantasy and whimsy," he says, "but it's probably too crazy for most people." In any event, he's glad to report that he currently has a steady girlfriend, a woman who works as a creative director and lives in Rhode Island. On one of those metal shelves sits a large gift-wrapped box that's tied with lavender satin ribbon and contained the Hermès umbrella she gave Mr. Chung for his birthday. The couple have been dating for a year, and he's optimistic about their prospects.

# 3

## Very Bushwick and Very Fabulous

Ben Shapiro and His Friends in Bushwick, Brooklyn

JULY 18, 2010

Ben Shapiro, a 26-year-old drummer and film student, with friends in a former beer baron's mansion in Bushwick, Brooklyn. (Benjamin Norman for *The New York Times*)

A CENTURY ago, when the Bushwick section of Brooklyn reigned as a center of the American brewing industry, a beer baron likely lived in the prim black-and-white mansion topped with a steeple on Bushwick Avenue; at least that's what local historians believe. But even in his wildest dreams, this Victorian captain of industry would never have envisioned how much the stately old place would rock a hundred years later.

He would never have imagined that nine artistically inclined 20-somethings—"Renaissance men and women," as they were once described—would use the premises to create hipper-than-thou music and art. He would never have imagined that crowds would pack the family manse for an installation called *When All through the House*, for which video screens projecting ghostly images flickered in every room. Or that a black-metal band called Liturgy would blast away in the musty, low-ceilinged basement, surrounded by an army of amps and dozens of dead Christmas trees. (Don't ask; it's a concept.) Or that a young math genius named Morgan Silver-Greenberg would be ensconced in the apartment in the steeple and that visitors to the house would trip over the flotilla of bikes and skateboards parked in the once sedate foyer.

Bushwick may not exactly be East Williamsburg, as real estate brokers like to describe the area. For people seeking the newest Bohemia, however, this neighborhood is arguably the coolest place on the planet. And in this epicenter of hip, few places are cooler than the white brick building with black trim that its residents call Cedar House, courtesy of its location on the corner of Cedar Street.

Given the house's slightly decrepit state, some locals are under the impression that the place is abandoned. The parents of the young men and women who live here might regard both the premises and the neighborhood as slightly squalid. But for Ben Shapiro's generation, the question is, How fast can I sign up?

"Really, there's nothing like this house anywhere in Brooklyn," says Mr. Shapiro, an original resident and the one who provides much of the glue that holds the place together. "Everyone's so creative and so talented. We're all friends, and this is such a fun place to play music." Not to mention the fact that in a city with a paucity of the garages and basements that have spawned countless bands, an entire floor in which to practice and perform is an almost undreamed-of luxury.

Mr. Shapiro, the son of two musically inclined parents from Providence, is 26, and like most of his housemates, he has a lot going on. After graduating from Sarah Lawrence, he spent two years touring the world as a drummer for a band called Asobi Seksu (the name is a colloquial Japanese term for playful sex). He also toured with a hardcore band called the Fugue, although one drug- and violence-soaked night when the Fugue was performing in Spiceland, Indiana, made him wonder whether living the rock-and-roll life full-time was really for him. At this point he decided to go to graduate school.

These days, along with completing work for a master's degree in film history at the Tisch School of the Arts at New York University and drumming with the bands Scary Mansion and Chris Garneau, Mr. Shapiro works part-time at Film Forum, the venerable downtown art house. If you've ever seen a dark-haired young man scooping popcorn at the concession stand while waiting for a Godard marathon to start, that would be him.

Thanks to an intimate knowledge of Brooklyn's music scene, notably venues of what Mr. Shapiro describes as "questionable legal status," he also contributes to *The New Yorker*'s pop music listings. "Plus," he points out as he conducts a little tour of the mansion, which dates back to 1901 and sometimes looks it, "living here is a job in itself."

The house's current incarnation began three years ago when Mr. Shapiro and a few friends who wanted to live together discovered the building and, despite the considerable disrepair, recognized its potential. People have come and gone, but as of last fall, the current lineup of residents, each of whom has a bedroom and pays about $600 in rent, was largely complete.

On the first floor live Morgan Jones, an artist; Jackie Oberman, a magazine graphic designer who plays bass in a punk band called the Homewreckers; and Lauren Denitzio, a freelance illustrator, graphic designer, and member of a punk band called the Measure. Also on the first floor: Hunter Hunt-Hendrix, the moving force behind Liturgy and a musician who likes to talk about the harmonic similarities between black metal and Brahms, and Mr. Shapiro, whose room features leather-bound copies of Balzac from an old girlfriend and, like nearly all the other bedrooms, tons of vinyl.

Upstairs live Danielle Rosa, a freelance art handler and social work student; Ben Keller, a video editor; and Julia Norton, an artist and musician. Ms. Norton's space, with its flowered curtains, sewing box, and collection of tiny enameled spoons, has the cluttered charm of a little girl's room, although few such rooms would house figurines clustered to represent such disasters as the Triangle shirtwaist factory fire. Her furnishings include half a dozen ukuleles, which she plays when she performs as half of the folk duo Paps, beloved for what one listener described as lullabies tinged with bluegrass. The steeple apartment is occupied by Mr. Silver-Greenberg, an installation artist who was such a star at N.Y.U.'s Gallatin School that in describing his prize-winning computer research, the school noted it was "easy to forget he's only 23."

In the basement are two art studios, plus the music studio and performance space that in many ways are the building's heart, or as Mr. Shapiro says of his reaction when he first saw the basement, "This was it for me." Concerts, which are generally free, are held here once a month, and some nights the crowds are so thick that they spill out the doors, with a couple hundred people flooding the second-floor terrace, the front lawn, and the sprawling backyard.

Many of the mansion's original architectural details have survived the years, among them transoms, window seats, wooden shutters, and stained-glass lighting fixtures that dangle from 10-foot ceilings. But even people who love the building most would hardly describe its condition as pristine. Floors are pockmarked with holes. Ceilings leak. It's easy to trip on the rickety steps that lead up to the steeple and down to the basement. "And keeping the place reasonably clean is an unbelievably huge challenge," Mr. Shapiro admits. "We have just a little money, and we try so hard to keep everyone happy."

Interpersonal relations are equally ticklish. One housemate left because of the noise; another was kicked out. "In a place like this," Mr. Shapiro says, "it's all out there. People's personalities become a house issue."

So does personal safety. The once solid middle-class neighborhood, which sagged badly during the 1960s, was devastated by the blackout of 1977. Looting started minutes after the lights went out, and mobs raced down Broadway, the main drag, "like a herd of buffalo," as a bystander described the scene. Fires raged as bullets, bricks, and bottles rained from the rooftops. Thirty blocks of Broadway were laid waste overnight; by the time the violence stopped, no stores were left to loot. Bushwick ultimately lost 20 percent of its housing stock, and the lifeblood of the neighborhood drained away. The story of Bushwick's destruction was one of the horrifying stories of the decade.

Even today, despite recently acquired hipster cachet, the streets aren't especially safe. Three people were murdered in the neighborhood last month, one of them on Bushwick Avenue, just blocks from Cedar House.

"It's still rough around the edges," Mr. Shapiro says of the area. "You have to keep your wits about you, like you do anywhere. But I feel safe. And I love it here, I really do. Plus the neighborhood is amazing. There's so much culture—there's night life, art, music, shows."

He sometimes thinks back, not with affection, to apartments of his recent past. "I've lived in these tiny, crummy, nothing places, these windowless boxes," he says, his eyes glazing over momentarily as he remembers one particularly heinous railroad apartment in Greenpoint. "Because usually that's the only thing you can afford." Here, by contrast, there's much to savor, not only the modest rent, the studio space, and the outdoor areas but also the rich history and the generous light, thanks to the profusion of tall windows. In the morning, Mr. Shapiro likes to sit on the front porch, furnished with sagging, mismatched chairs, the stuffing oozing out of the sofa, as he eats breakfast and reads the newspaper while trucks barrel down Bushwick Avenue. The experience, as a blogger once said of a Cedar House event, is "very Bushwick and very fabulous."

# 4

# Southern Shimmer

## Daniel and Dasha Faires on the Lower East Side

NOVEMBER 29, 2010

Daniel and Dasha Faires, 20-something transplants from Arkansas, in their 375-square-foot apartment on the Lower East Side. (Nicole Bengiveno/*The New York Times*)

To reach the apartment where Daniel and Dasha Faires live, you pass through the vestibule of a small brick building on Ludlow Street and head down a dingy hallway edged with grimy blue and white tile. There's little evidence that anyone lives on this floor, or even that much has happened since this building was erected a century earlier. But hang a left at the end of the passageway near the trash can, and you'll find something amazing.

This is the Lilliputian home where the Faireses, newlyweds from Arkansas in their mid-20s, have lived for the past year. Both work in fields that demand visual flair—she's a sales representative for BB Dakota, a moderately priced line of women's fashions; he builds furniture and owns a design firm that bears his name—and together they've created an exquisite space in which a good eye trumps minimal square footage.

The ground-floor apartment, which they rent for $2,000 a month, has just two rooms, a bedroom and an everything-else room. Their home is so small that when the Faireses were married last summer back in Arkansas, the wedding invitation instructed guests wondering what to give the happy couple to "please remember that they live in a 375-square-foot apartment in New York City." Yet despite the diminutive size, and though the rooms are dark even at midday, the space shimmers, thanks to artfully placed mirrors, votive candles deployed with a lavish hand, and incandescent Edison bulbs whose golden filaments glisten like giant fireflies. Gauzy white tulle curtains conceal windows that face brick walls and dreary alleyways. "To be honest," Ms. Faires says, "it's sort of like a cave in here because the only natural light comes from the backyard. But fortunately, we love the dark."

The Faireses are part of the seemingly endless stream of young people from around the country and around the world who make their way to New York in hopes of achieving glory or at least a more interesting life than the one they left behind. Although some triumph, many more flounder, unable to establish a personal or professional toehold, especially in a time of punishing housing costs and pervasive unemployment. Reluctantly, they return to the place from which they came, muttering bitterly about the impossibility of making a life for themselves in the city. But the Faireses were among the lucky ones. They had each other, they found work that suited them, and they have transformed a space that some people would find as confining as a coffin into a shiny jewel box.

The two have been a couple ever since they were set up, sort of, for their high school homecoming dance in 1999. "I would say we hit the ground running," Mr. Faires says. Not that the relationship didn't have its moments. "In the beginning," he recalls, "we fought like cats and dogs. We've been together for 11 years, and we still fight like we're 15."

By 2006, they had made their way to a fifth-floor walk-up in Hoboken, New Jersey, on the other side of the Hudson River, and within a couple of years, to New York. While their current apartment could be tucked into their old bedroom in Hoboken and many people would balk at the rent, Mr. Faires regards their home as a find. The location is a major draw, especially for someone like him, who uses wood salvaged from the street to build his furniture and for whom the Lower East Side is an ideal hunting ground. "And this apartment offers so much," his wife says. "The exposed brick walls, the high ceilings, the wood and marble floors. The ambience was here even before we moved in."

Ambience there was to spare. And the Faireses added considerable dollops of their own, starting with the chalkboard that covers an entire wall. Mr. Faires, who created the board using matte black paint, describes it as "very fun and very durable," and everyone who visits leaves a calling card. "Ant wuz here," wrote Ms. Faires's cousin Anthony, who is serving in Iraq. Someone scribbled the first verse of Lao Tzu's *Tao Te Ching*. There's a jotting in Japanese and the words "I love Hot Grits," a reference to Ms. Faires's band, whose name is an acronym for "girls raised in the South." Someone drew a candy cane during last year's 1940s-themed Christmas party, at which 50 guests—the men in trench coats and fedoras, the women in long dresses—smoked cigars or skinny cigarettes and dined on shoofly pie and apple pandowdy. "But nothing dirty or profane," Mr. Faires says of the writing on the wall. "We only like happy things."

Along with attracting party guests, the apartment is a magnet for longer-term visitors. At least once a month, visitors bed down on what Mr. Faires calls "this measly little futon from Ikea," a piece that opens into a queen-sized bed and is dressed by day in a white bed skirt and matching pillows meant to evoke Colonial America. "We're the go-to place," he says. "It's exhausting, but we love it."

When the couple moved in, they ate their meals perched on the futon, balancing their plates on their laps. Now they use the table and benches that Mr. Faires made from wood he found in Hell's Kitchen, "a pile of wood," he says, "that was heavy on my heart." The table and benches are part of his furniture line, Capsule Furniture, a company that takes its name from the glass capsule tucked inside each piece containing observations on the wood's history.

Thanks to the Faireses' taste for repurposing, even mundane items enjoy a second act. Mail is kept in a metal bicycle basket. Mr. Faires stores his tools in an ancient black trunk that doubles as a table. And thanks especially to his design skills, nothing seems ordinary. Open shelves hold wine glasses, white mugs, and soup bowls, most of them bought from big-box stores like Ikea but so artfully arranged they look as if they belonged in a museum. Mr. Faires designed and built a spice rack that also looks like a museum-quality piece, a lattice of two dozen glass tubes, each filled with a different ingredient. "Whatever you wake up and are inspired by," says Mr. Faires, who grew up in an old house and describes the Dumpster as his best friend, "that's what you make." His wife calls him the dreamer.

Their bedroom faces the garden, where coils of razor wire and the yowl of the stray cats that live in the alley—the Faireses have named them Jade, Gimpy, and Tomcat and describe them as very sweet—reminds them that the neighborhood retains its rough edges. But the garden is also idyllic, especially at night, when Moroccan lanterns and strands of bistro lights prick the darkness. Even on the chilliest evenings, the couple and their guests hang out here, facing a table with bicycle wheels for legs and sitting on benches that Mr. Faires built from shipping crates. And even in this most urban of neighborhoods, the garden is unexpectedly lush. Mr. Faires, whose passion for landscaping is almost as great as his passion for furniture making, has planted Virginia creeper, creeping Jenny, and autumn stonecrop, along with the honeysuckle and sweet potato vine beloved in his native South.

Sitting there one late autumn night, Ms. Faires wearing a black maxi skirt, a wide-brimmed black felt hat over her long blond hair, and a necklace hung with a tintype and a skeleton key, her bearded husband in Levis from the Goodwill in Nashville ($3.99 a pair) and a bracelet he made from twine and vintage trinkets, the two resembled characters from the 19th-century ambrotype that hangs in their living room. And their small world seemed vast. "Do I feel the walls closing in?" Ms. Faires says. "Not me. The apartment is so cozy, all I feel is a feeling of warmth."

# Starting Over

# 5

# The House of Open Arms

## Filipp and Raya Katz in Bath Beach, Brooklyn

**FEBRUARY 7, 2010**

Filipp and Raya Katz, Russian émigrés, who live in a split-level house in Bath Beach, Brooklyn. (Kirsten Luce for *The New York Times*)

THE journey that brought Filipp and Raya Katz to the red-brick and beige-stone house that Ms. Katz calls "my little palace" began more than half a century ago in the Ukrainian city of Mukachevo, near the Hungarian border. The Katzes grew up on the same street, not far from the river that runs through the city, and they knew each other as children. A sorrowful bond was the fact that all four of their parents had been Holocaust survivors.

Their story resumed two decades later in Israel. Mr. Katz, who by then had immigrated to the United States, paid a visit to that country and reconnected with his former childhood friend, who had settled there. By 1983, they were married. In a wedding photograph that sits behind the sofa in their living room, the dark-haired, dark-eyed newlyweds gaze beatifically from the heart of a red rose. "A little kitsch," Ms. Katz says with an unapologetic smile.

For many years after moving to the United States, the couple and their son, Nathan, now a 23-year-old teacher's assistant, lived in a small semi-attached house in Kensington, Brooklyn, near Mr. Katz's parents. But they knew something of the world that lay beyond their front door. Avid cyclists, they regularly climbed aboard their Treks, pulled on their helmets (hers was silver, his white), and pedaled off to the shoreline bike path that runs under the Verrazano-Narrows Bridge and along Gravesend Bay. From that vantage point, they looked longingly at the houses in Bath Beach, a community that hugs the borough's southwestern tip. "I used to say, it's my dream to live close to the water," Ms. Katz says, "and in a free-standing house."

By 2003, with both of Mr. Katz's parents dead, little remained to tether the younger generation to the old neighborhood. One chilly spring morning in 2007, when they were in Bath Beach checking out a house on Cropsey Avenue, Ms. Katz's eye was caught by a '60s-era split-level across the street. In its little rear garden, bushes were starting to explode with bright orange buds. "That's the one I want," she announced. Her husband, who was especially taken with the brick accents on the façade, a reminder of the building material so familiar from his childhood, felt the same way. "Even outside," he recalls, "I said to myself, 'We're home.'" At that point, they hadn't set foot past the front door.

The Katzes had arrived in Bath Beach at an opportune moment. For generations, the area had been home to Jews and Italians; neighboring

Bensonhurst had been the setting for the 1977 movie *Saturday Night Fever*, one of the iconic portraits of outer-borough New York and, less happily, the place where a black teenager named Yusuf Hawkins was fatally beaten by a gang of white youths in 1989 when he came to the area to look at a used car. In recent years, families from China, Russia, Mexico, and the Middle East have been streaming into the neighborhood. As old-timers began moving away, their one- and two-family houses, among them the dwelling that so charmed the Katzes, were coming onto the market.

The four-bedroom house, which they bought for about $800,000, sits sandwiched snugly between two other homes. High-rises tower across the street. The house might not suit everyone, nor would the blindingly bright décor be to everyone's taste. Yet it would be difficult to find a couple more enamored of the place where they live. And for two people whose parents had escaped death in the concentration camps, who themselves grew up amid the privations of postwar Russia, and who started out, as Mr. Katz sums it up, "with nothing," it's understandable that a place that offered both emotional roots and physical comfort would be meaningful.

A main attraction was the downstairs apartment that's now home to the couple's son. Another was the convenience of the neighborhood, especially for Mr. Katz, who works for a local social services organization and volunteers at the Shore Parkway Jewish Center, a nearby synagogue. A third was that the house, whose longtime owners were retiring to New Jersey, needed virtually nothing in the way of renovation, although its pristine condition did not prevent the couple from putting their stamp on the premises with considerable brio. "It's like appetite," Mr. Katz says, using a simile that one suspects would sound even more vivid in his native Russian. "It grows when you eat."

Over the next three years, the Katzes embarked on one project after another, among them creating a space in the basement where Ms. Katz, who's an aesthetician, can give facials to friends and relatives. She herself designed her bathroom, whose walls are sheathed in snowy Italian ceramic embossed with images of nymphs and goddesses. Next on their to-do list, the kitchen, a relic of the era in which coal-black appliances and countertops were the epitome of chic.

Everywhere there are reminders of the fact that for the first time in their life, this couple, now in their mid-50s, can indulge themselves. Notable in this regard are the mirrored cabinets that line the walls of Mr. Katz's dressing room and are stuffed with dozens, perhaps hundreds, of shirts, sweaters, and other garments. Many purchases nestle in their original cellophane packages, never opened.

According to Ms. Katz, the roots of this passion for haberdashery run deep. "He loves clothes, and he always dreamed of being a good dresser," she says of her husband. "But when he was young, it was hard to get anything. Here in America, we could afford to buy. So he can't stop buying." How many items are stored in this generous space? "I have no idea," she says. "We never counted." Out of earshot of her husband, she murmurs, "I think we're afraid to count."

Another touch of luxury is the handmade Italian chess set on a cabinet in the dining area. The board, which rests on little feet, is made of squares of red- and cream-colored wood, and the exquisitely crafted silver chess pieces, studded with flecks of red ceramic, bear distinctly Slavic features. The set comes from a store in Borough Park that sells silver Judaica, one Mr. Katz used to pass when his parents lived nearby, and he found the item so alluring, he used to dream about it. Ms. Katz, who bought the set as a present for her husband's 57th birthday and the couple's 25th wedding anniversary, whispers the price out of his hearing: "A thousand dollars."

Also quite luxurious is the gargantuan entertainment unit that dominates the living room, its centerpiece a 42-inch television set topped with silver cups and candlesticks. "All are from the old country," Ms. Katz says. "The candelabra, which was in my husband's family, survived after the war. But the parents didn't have a single picture of the grandparents."

The couple are immensely fond of a large and colorful oil titled *Drunk in the Garden*, painted by a close friend named Frank Engels, who created a similar work for their bedroom. And this house, unlike that of Mr. Katz's parents, is home to a profusion of family photographs, depicting among other things the Katzes in Halloween costumes, she as a Spanish dancer, he as a dashing young officer; his father, in a prayer shawl and yarmulke at the synagogue; and the couple's son, age 3, wearing a jaunty red bowtie.

Although the Katzes have put many aspects of their past behind them, their house is dotted with reminders of their native Mukachevo, including a picture of its city hall on the refrigerator and, on a nearby wall, a plate depicting the local fortress set against the mountains that ring the city. A trio of paintings show Mukachevo in winter, summer, and fall (spring somehow disappeared). The images remind the couple of their roots but even more of how far they've come. "For immigrants to get something like this," Ms. Katz says of the house, "it's a dream come true. You love it like you love a person." Her husband expresses it another way. "It makes you believe that life is beautiful," he says.

# 6

## Her Cottage by the Sea

### Amy Gottlieb and Her Family on City Island

FEBRUARY 28, 2010

Amy Gottlieb, a special education teacher, and her children in a 1920s cottage on City Island in the Bronx. (Chester Higgins Jr./*The New York Times*)

WHEN the towers fell, Amy Gottlieb was in the kitchen of her family's Battery Park City apartment, serving breakfast to her twin daughters, not yet a year old. Ms. Gottlieb, a special education teacher, and her husband, Terry McElroy, an artist, had rented the apartment only three months earlier, attracted by the complex's child-friendly vibes. Just the previous morning, Ms. Gottlieb had begun sharing a babysitter with a mother of twins who lived nearby.

By 12:30 on that brilliant blue-sky day, Ms. Gottlieb had packed up her daughters in the double stroller, scooped up Mishka, her chow chow, along with baby formula on ice, and was aboard a boat headed to New Jersey. Except for the twins and the dog, she was alone, and she had no idea what was happening back in the apartment. "We were told they weren't letting husbands back in the building," she says. Nor did she ever set foot in the apartment again. When Mr. McElroy returned a few weeks later to collect their belongings, the remains of breakfast still sat on the kitchen table.

Ms. Gottlieb did not lose family or friends in the attacks. She was not sickened by the grime-filled air or permanently traumatized by the violence of that day. But like so many New Yorkers, she can recount in practically moment-by-moment detail what happened in the minutes and hours after the towers were hit. Her description of the remains of the family's breakfast recalls one of the most moving images to emerge after the attacks, the photograph of a tea set blanketed with white dust that was found in an apartment near Ground Zero. And because she was living in the shadow of the towers, amid the debris and the seemingly endless physical disruption, her life and her family's was upended.

Also like so many New Yorkers whose domestic arrangements were convulsed on September 11, 2001, the couple instantly faced the question of where to go next, a question complicated by the presence of two babies. For a time they camped out in her parents' apartment on the Upper East Side. But finding permanent housing in Manhattan proved financially daunting, especially given the modesty of their respective salaries. And despite Ms. Gottlieb's affection for Rockaway, the waterfront community in Queens where she grew up, she had no desire to return to the streets of her youth. She did, however, respond to the siren song of another close-knit neighborhood encircled by water, City Island in the

Bronx. "It felt very comfortable, like the Rockaways," she says. "That was a major plus."

The family moved to the island in 2002, living for a time in a rented apartment. Yet almost from the beginning, Ms. Gottlieb and her husband began to look for something more permanent, and she took a liking to a two-story-plus-attic candy-pink house with daffodil-yellow shutters. From the shrubbery garlanding the front porch to the oculus and stained-glass windows, the place exuded old-fashioned charm even though it had been erected well into the 20th century. That the house sat just steps from Eastchester Bay was an added attraction; Ms. Gottlieb, perhaps thanks to her Rockaway youth, loved the idea of living so close to the water. She was also enamored of the log-burning fireplace in the living room and the wallpaper in the dining room, with birds and flowers worked in a palette of gold, maroon, brown, and green. "This house had a history," she says. "I fell in love with everything about it."

Not until a year later would the price fall to a level the couple could afford. "I kept looking at other houses," she says, "but I was determined to wait for this one." In 2003, she and her husband bought the house for about $570,000; their son, Julian, was born the following year. Yet period charm failed to prove a recipe for domestic contentment. Two years ago, after eight years of marriage, the couple separated. Mr. McElroy now lives near the New York Botanical Garden—off island, as the locals say; this is a community in which geography is everything.

Yet Ms. Gottlieb, who is now 46, is still enamored of her cottage by the sea. Although she has made various changes—"I cleaned it up quite a bit" is how she describes the elimination of some of the froufrou—the house retains much of its original character, along with decorative items that speak to an earlier and more gracious era.

When it came to furnishings, Ms. Gottlieb proved a catalogue publisher's dream. Nearly every purchase came from one of the dozens of publications that flooded her mailbox: Restoration Hardware, Home Decorators, West Elm, Smith & Noble—you name it, she found something in its pages that spoke to her. "Whatever came, I just looked through it and bought what I liked," she recalls. "Very mix and match. I'm not fussy." She made many of the decorating decisions the summer after Julian was born, leafing through all those catalogues as she sat on the couch next to her mother.

The wallpaper in the dining room, as pristine as the day it was hung, proved so alluring that Ms. Gottlieb echoed its palette throughout the first floor. In the living room, gold velvet drapes loop over filmy white lace curtains, and the claw-foot sofa is upholstered in a chocolaty brocade. On one wall hangs a photograph, complete with an ornate gilded frame, of a girl with an enormous white bow in her hair; Ms. Gottlieb bought the picture at a City Island shop called Early Ruth Antiques, original home of many of the works of art that dress up her rooms.

Despite her love of period details, some remnants of the original décor have bitten the dust. Ms. Gottlieb got rid of the window seats, scrapped the shutters, and repainted the exterior a more subdued shade of pink. In the kitchen, she retained the ceramic tiles embossed with images of fruit, but decorative accents now include her collection of vintage lunch boxes, honoring such blasts from the past as *Welcome Back, Kotter* and *Charlie's Angels*. Elsewhere, too, Ms. Gottlieb has exercised a little stylistic license. While one porch is furnished with tasteful green wicker, another is outfitted with a leopard-print rug and gold faux-suede upholstery that would have amazed, though possibly delighted, the house's original occupants.

Amid the old-fashioned décor there's ample evidence that three young children are in residence. Classic board games such as Sorry! and Othello are stuffed into the bookshelves in the living room. In the bedroom occupied by the twins, Phoebe and Lydia, steel and glass desks sit side by side. Julian has his own room, proclaimed by a pillow bearing his name in block letters. In the basement are two playrooms: the pine-paneled one and what Ms. Gottlieb calls "the messy activity one." Come warmer weather, the children will relocate to the backyard, where in a few months forsythia and wisteria will be in bloom.

Ms. Gottlieb also provided design perks for herself, reconfiguring the second floor to create a walk-in closet, along with a master bathroom with a claw-foot tub. She's so enchanted with her attic, she insists that a visitor climb the narrow, pull-down ladder to see how much room she has up there to store out-of-season clothes.

If you ran into Ms. Gottlieb on the street, perhaps peering into the window of Early Ruth Antiques, you might wonder if she's sorry she left Manhattan. The other day, outfitted in layers of gray with matching leggings and slouchy suede boots, her burgundy nails perfectly manicured, her long bangs perfectly cut, she looked as if she had wandered over from the chic precincts of the Condé Nast cafeteria.

Unlike so many City Islanders, she doesn't own a boat; boats make her seasick. She has, however, plunged enthusiastically into island affairs. She's active in the work of the City Island Community Center and, even more than she might have anticipated, is savoring the small-town feel and feeling warmly welcomed. "I've felt very comfortable here," Ms. Gottlieb says. She admits that she's hardly a clam digger, the local term for people born on the island. "I'm very Manhattanish," she says. "But I feel I've been embraced as a local."

# 7

## Here I Am. And Here We Are.

### Robbin Brosterman and Benno Schoberth in Lenox Hill

JULY 25, 2010

Robbin Brosterman and her new husband, Benno Schoberth, in her longtime studio in Lenox Hill. (Susan Farley for *The New York Times*)

DECADES before Carrie Bradshaw settled into her apartment in an East Side brownstone, the neighborhood was a mecca for young single women seeking a taste of the big city. And among the legions drawn to the area over the years was a 21-year-old design-school graduate named Robbin Brosterman, who in 1980 moved to a one-bedroom apartment on East 57th Street. "A teacher of mine at Fashion Institute of Technology used to say that you never really knew the city until you lived in Manhattan," explains Ms. Brosterman, who had grown up in Marine Park, a Brooklyn neighborhood where the subway signs to Manhattan said simply, "To the city." "All I ever wanted was to be part of it."

Within a few years, she was ensconced in another rental, this one in Lenox Hill, a 475-square-foot alcove studio on 70th Street near Second Avenue. Around 1985, when the building was poised to go co-op, her mother, Dorothy, issued a directive. "I want you to own something," she told her daughter firmly. Along with Ms. Brosterman's grandmother, a onetime corset model named Etta Walker, the mother followed up with a very tempting and concrete incentive. Together, the two women gave Ms. Brosterman small sums of money that allowed her to make a down payment on the Lenox Hill studio, which was priced at $62,000.

Ms. Brosterman is charmed by this story, as she is charmed by many stories. "I always loved the fact that it was two women who made this possible," she says. She furnished the place with golden oak antiques because "in those days, everyone bought golden oak." The décor also included a set of turn-of-the-century gilded ballroom chairs that her guests never sat on for fear that they might break.

Over the years, as her friends bounced from one place to another, Ms. Brosterman stayed put. After a series of arts-related jobs, she ended up as design director at DC Entertainment, formerly DC Comics, despite the fact that she had never read a comic book in her life. She also did her share of online dating. Then, around Christmas 2006, in one of her forays into the world of online romance, she met a German-born film editor named Benno Schoberth who was living on the top floor of a two-family house in Williamsburg.

Mr. Schoberth, born in the German city of Aachen, had moved to Berlin as a young man. But after his older brother visited New York and raved about the city, Mr. Schoberth promptly bought a round-trip ticket and was so smitten by the place that shortly after his arrival in 1986 he ceremoniously tore up the return portion.

When Mr. Schoberth arrived in New York, he was 25, knew only high school English, and had just a few hundred dollars to his name. Armed with a gently doctored résumé, he bluffed his way into a job as an apprentice film editor and gradually forged a career as a film and television editor, educating himself about American popular culture through his work on A&E biographies of such figures as the disco impresario Steve Rubell. He also worked on a PBS film about the trials of Adolph Eichmann, poring for months over footage that, as a member of Germany's first postwar generation, he found enormously moving. In addition, he wrote and directed an award-winning film called *Shelter*, a story of poor urban teenagers who break into a secluded beach house.

When Mr. Schoberth and Ms. Brosterman connected online, he was 45, she was 47, and the chemistry between the Brooklyn hipster with the shaven head and the effervescent strawberry blonde from the Upper East Side was instantaneous. "He wrote me an email that was the rightest email I'd ever gotten," Ms. Brosterman recalls. "I could tell he was a good soul."

Slightly more than a year later, on February 13, 2008, the two decided to move in together. The following day, Valentine's Day, fate offered an extra nudge. Mr. Schoberth's landlord informed him that the building in which he had been living for a decade was about to be razed and replaced with an apartment house. As a result, the studio where Ms. Brosterman had lived for nearly a quarter of a century allowed the couple to write the next chapter of their lives. Three weeks later, Mr. Schoberth arrived with his things.

The move was not without angst, at least on his part. "It was a grand experiment for both of us, especially living in one room," admits Mr. Schoberth, who kept some of his furniture in storage in case the arrangement didn't work out. "But at a certain point you figure, just do it. Don't play it safe. And you come out the other end, and you're in a really good place." Four months later, the two were married at City Hall, and over the past two years, they've merged their possessions and their lives, reconfiguring the studio and jointly buying many pieces of contemporary furniture and original works of art.

Their bed is a reproduction of a midcentury Case Study platform bed manufactured by Modernica, a low slab perched on delicate feet that is covered with cheerful orange and white spreads. They dine on a Frank Gehry Face Off café table, a slab of glass atop braided ribbons of maple.

And virtually every item represents a shared moment in their relationship. The blue and green cartoonlike painting by Jesse Reno of Portland, Oregon, was a present from Ms. Brosterman to Mr. Schoberth on their first anniversary. The Kenny Scharf woodcut of a blue and green monster was a wedding present from friends. Above the dining table hangs a luminous white lighting fixture made of paper and wood glue, the work of a French designer named Céline Wright; the couple had seen the fixture in a clothing store during a trip to Paris, inquired as to whether it was for sale, and ended up meeting its creator. As a couple, they commissioned the fluffy, origami-like sculpture by Max Steiner made of a single sheet of folded paper. Together they bought the marigold rug, the curvy bamboo coffee table, and the brushed-nickel lamps by Sonneman Orbiter.

Interspersed with all the cutting-edge art are decorative items carrying strong family associations. The crystal Orrefors vase that has been a fixture in the apartment for decades came from Ms. Brosterman's mother. The aluminum candlesticks made by a cousin of Mr. Schoberth's had been in his mother's apartment. "Moose in the Tropics," a block of clear plastic in which is embedded a miniature moose surrounded by baby palm trees, was made by Ms. Brosterman's older brother Norman as a Sweet 16 gift to his sister.

The décor also includes nods to one of the women without whom Ms. Brosterman wouldn't be in this apartment today. Near the front door hangs a photograph of Ms. Brosterman's grandmother, who worked for the Nemo Corset Company in the 1920s and is pictured with her co-workers wearing Nemo's signature creation over their dresses. A newspaper ad published in 1912, advertising the company's spring lines of corsets, hangs on another wall. The ad was a gift for Ms. Brosterman's 40th birthday, and as someone who believes in signs and portents, she's much taken with the fact that the newspaper is dated March 31, her birthday.

Ms. Brosterman treasures the family memorabilia, but her favorite decorative touch looks to the future. She finds something almost mystical about the speed and ease with which she and Mr. Schoberth became a couple, and she sees as a symbol of their relationship the laser-cut glass-and-steel room divider that he built when they moved in together. To make the divider, Mr. Schoberth taught himself to weld, and this piece, which separates the living and sleeping areas and is studded with orbs of clear handblown glass, is the thing they love most in the apartment.

The room divider figures prominently in Ms. Brosterman's account of how the couple met and created a life together, a story you suspect she has told countless times, each time with the same gusto. "Basically," she says, "this is about a girl from Brooklyn who spent years looking for love, travel, and art and a guy who came to New York looking for his 'true life' and the 'real thing' and found it in each other and in our 475-square-foot studio with our apartment jewel, our room divider." Again and again, she marvels at the role the studio has played in their relationship. "I never expected to remain in such a small space for so long," she says. "I always thought I'd be in someplace bigger. But here I am. And here we are."

# Living with Ghosts

# 8

## The House That Saved His Life

### Peter Marchette and His Family in Long Island City, Queens

**AUGUST 9, 2009**

Peter Marchette and his daughter, son-in-law, and grandsons in their apartment house in Long Island City, Queens. (G. Paul Burnett/*The New York Times*)

PETER Marchette and Julia Walsh of Long Island City, Queens, were the ultimate childhood sweethearts. They met in 1958, when he was 7 and she was 5, in a neighborhood whose mostly working-class residents were bound by family ties and often by roots that went back to the same Italian town or Irish village.

"We met right here in this yard," Mr. Marchette says, sitting in the backyard of the three-story apartment house on 47th Road where he grew up. By 1965, the two were going steady, and in 1971, when he was 20 and she was 18, they were married at St. Mary's Roman Catholic Church, just around the corner. Their son, Peter Jr., was born later that year, and a daughter, Victoria, followed in 1977. Within a few years of living elsewhere in the neighborhood, the family was back on 47th Road, in an apartment on the first floor.

For the most part, New York is a place of relentless change, a place where people move about at warp speed. But just below the surface there lies a different New York. The story of this house and its inhabitants over the years sheds a rare light on that other New York, a world of countless small residential buildings in immigrant neighborhoods, buildings that stay for decades in one extended family, with multiple generations living under the same roof. Nearly from the moment this house was built, around 1870, it was owned or occupied by Mr. Marchette's relatives or members of his wife's family. And three years ago, when his wife died suddenly of a heart attack at the age of 53, the house came to his rescue.

Mr. Marchette still lives on the first floor, where he lived when his wife was alive. His daughter, along with her husband, Anthony Voss, and the couple's sons, Anthony William Jr., 4, and Zachary, 10 months, moved into the four-room railroad flat on the top floor. And while Mr. Marchette is still picking up the pieces after the death of his wife, the presence of these four cheerful people under his roof may have saved his life. "Without them," he says, "I probably would have folded up my tent a long time ago. I would have gone into the tank." His voice shakes as he speaks.

For Ms. Voss, the arrangement has proved equally comforting. Thanks to her father, she was able to return to her job as a preschool teacher shortly after the birth of her younger son. Her father, who is 58, had recently been laid off from his job as a customer service representative for a French wine importer, and she asked if he would be her babysitter. He was reluctant, afraid he wouldn't be much good at what he always considered women's work. "A woman knows these things instinctively," Mr. Marchette said to his daughter of the challenges involved. "I can only try." Yet despite his misgivings, he proved a natural. "He's a wonderful grandfather," his daughter says. "When he's with the baby, I have peace of mind."

Mr. Voss, who grew up in Greenpoint, just across the Brooklyn-Queens border, and whose parents were divorced when he was a teenager, found a different sort of support within these four walls, a closeness he never experienced as a young boy. "Sitting in this chair," he says this day in the backyard, "I felt a warmth. I was closer to my mother-in-law than to my own mother. My father-in-law the same thing. They always told me they loved me."

Having grown children under the parental roof doesn't always work smoothly, as countless parents who have tried and abandoned the arrangement can attest. The closeness is too much. Parents try not to criticize their children, or the way the grandchildren are being raised, but biting one's tongue over and over can strain a relationship to the breaking point. Mercifully for Mr. Marchette, this multigenerational household has remarkably few sharp edges.

Like many of the old houses in Long Island City, this one has acquired modern conveniences—its earliest residents stoked a coal furnace and bathed in a tub in the kitchen—and the original scalloped brown wood shingles have made way for more up-to-date green siding. But even with recent improvements, the six small apartments, four of which are occupied by rental tenants, are modest. Despite recent gentrification, with one after another industrial building making way for new condominiums, many streets are still a motley mix of stores, factories, and small apartment houses like this one. And as with so many buildings in this neighborhood, the story of who lived here when is a complicated tale.

The first of Mr. Marchette's relatives to occupy the house was his maternal great-grandmother, Rosina Diccicio, who had emigrated from Italy with her parents. Shortly after the house was built, she rented an apartment on the third floor from a family named Tassa, the building's owners. Rosina's daughter—Nanny Rose, as everyone called her—was born in the house around 1900 and lived in the same second-floor apartment. Her daughter, Delores, who was Mr. Marchette's mother, was born in the house, too, in 1928. In 1945, Delores's brother, John, bought the house from the Tassa family for about $4,000.

Mr. Marchette's parents lived in the house when he was growing up. His father, he says, "was in the dancing business," opening studios for Arthur Murray, and as a child, Peter remembers a lively if hectic neighborhood, with freight trains rumbling along the railroad tracks, trolley cars lurching down Vernon Boulevard, lumbering trucks, noisy factories.

In the early '70s, when the family moved to New Jersey, they sold the house for $39,000 to Mr. Marchette's mother-in-law, who promptly moved in. In 1993, she signed the house over to her son-in-law, although she remained in her first-floor apartment until her death three years ago, just five months before the death of her daughter. Mr. Marchette can't get over how lucky he was at such a difficult moment. "The house came back to me," Mr. Marchette says of the building. "What goes around comes around."

During warm weather, much of the family's life takes place in the backyard, which overflowed with roses when Mr. Marchette was a child and is now home to a huge above-ground pool and a gas grill. In cold weather, everyone retreats to the finished basement.

The apartments that branch off the narrow slate landings are snug and simple. Ceilings are low and closets few. Mr. Marchette's apartment is dominated by a big television set. "I treated myself," he explains.

The Vosses' apartment accommodates a crib for Zachary and a day-bed for Anthony William, with a curtain separating the children's room from their parents' bedroom. "There's not a lot of privacy," Ms. Voss admits. But she's not complaining. "When my mother and my grandmother passed away," she says, "my father would have been totally alone. I'm glad I'm here and that we're all together."

# 9

# And for Compensation, the View

## Paul Moakley on Staten Island

DECEMBER 27, 2009

Paul Moakley, a photographer, in the historic Alice Austen House in Staten Island. (Hiroko Masuike for *The New York Times*)

TRUTH be told, life at the Alice Austen House on Staten Island was livelier back in the day, the day being the late 19th and early 20th centuries, when the building's namesake ruled the roost.

Austen, a product of the late-19th-century boom in serious amateur photography, was Staten Island's best-known practitioner of the art form, not to mention a rare woman in a field that in her era and beyond was almost entirely male. A familiar local figure, she lived in this Gothic Revival–style cottage, which faces a broad front lawn and commands a breathtaking view of Upper New York Bay. From here she used to set out for the ferry to Manhattan, there to capture images of fishmongers, bootblacks, and other working men and women whose occupations were considered decidedly déclassé. Nor were working-class New Yorkers the only subject that interested Austen. She also took pictures of the young men and women of her social set, at parties, playing sports, at the beach, on excursions. Photographs of her girlfriends jauntily smoking cigarettes in their nightclothes or dressed in vests and top hats reveal her sense of humor and her willingness to test the limits of propriety.

In 1985, the cottage where she had spent most of her life was bought by the city's Department of Parks and Recreation for use as a house museum, and today its rooms are visited by tourists and groups of schoolchildren. But if Austen were still in evidence—admittedly unlikely, given that she died in 1952 at the age of 86, Paul Moakley almost certainly wouldn't be occupying the snug little apartment on the cottage's top floor.

He wouldn't be able to gaze through the diamond-paned dormer windows as tankers and cruise ships glide in and out of the harbor. He wouldn't be roused at night by the sudden clank of a vessel dropping anchor. He wouldn't be able to watch hawks and cardinals as he washes dishes in his kitchen, a space as compact as a ship's galley and with appropriately slanting floorboards. He wouldn't be living with a ghost, albeit one for whom he feels a deep affinity.

Mr. Moakley, a photographer and photo editor who has served as the full-time caretaker and curator here for the past four years, is a dark-haired, soft-spoken 33-year-old seemingly possessed of none of the sharp elbows common in his profession. And like the house's namesake, he's a child of the island through and through. He has lived on the island since his family moved here from Queens when he was a baby, and he admits that he is seduced by the rhythms of island life.

The day after graduating from college, he and two friends rented a century-old house on Bay Street, just up the road from the museum, which is at 2 Hylan Boulevard. "It was the oldest, most decrepit house I could find," Mr. Moakley says as he settles into a rare unoccupied space on the living room sofa, surrounded by quantities of photographic paraphernalia. "I'd grown up in a duplex, and I always hated the place. I thought it was flimsy, and there was no privacy. It was definitely not cozy."

Mr. Moakley did something else the day after graduation. He got a job as a photo editor at a magazine called *PDN* (the initials stand for *Photo District News*), a job that reflected a longstanding passion. It wasn't an easy career to pursue, in part because when he was growing up, Mr. Moakley had no exposure to anyone who shared his interest in this world. "Everyone in my family worked in construction," he explains. "I didn't know anyone who had a nice camera."

As he was finding his way professionally, the Austen House held a particular allure. He often sat under a honey locust on the front lawn reading the newspaper. And though shyness made him uncomfortable in traditional galleries, he felt relaxed at the exhibitions held in these rooms.

In 2003, he curated a pair of photography exhibitions at the Austen museum, and two years later, when the previous caretaker left, Mr. Moakley was asked to replace him and move into his four-room apartment. The space includes the bedroom occupied for a time by Austen's Aunt Minn and Uncle Oswald, the man who gave Alice her first camera, and although Mr. Moakley doesn't say it in so many words, he seems moved by the fact that he's living in the longtime home of someone who shared his passion for this art form.

The furnishings are largely hand-me-downs and finds from the street. But these odds and ends inhabit a space made memorable by the profusion of period architectural details—sharply angled ceilings, secret cupboards, built-in shelves and cabinets, bookcases with glass doors, and wide floorboards crafted from the hulls of whaling ships that were broken apart upon arriving in the New World. These quarters seem an ideal place to curl up on a blustery night with a copy of *Moby Dick* and a mug of steaming tea or, better yet, a whisky.

The living room is dominated by a huge silkscreen of a sunset that Mr. Moakley's father, who liked to rescue discarded art from the buildings where he worked, found in an empty office. Vintage photographs of Mr. Moakley's family reflect his curiosity about the mysterious ways that place and past intertwine, and they echo a film and video project of his that he calls "Memory Loop." Mr. Moakley's father has Alzheimer's, and as he sinks deeper into dementia, the son thinks a great deal about the role of memory and the ravages of its disappearance.

The sun that streams through the unshuttered windows is so blinding that Mr. Moakley must sometimes move his bed to one side to avoid being awakened at dawn. But the light is one of the things he loves about the apartment, and as the sun travels across the sky, he finds each room beautiful in a different way.

Mr. Moakley is here because the Austen House, as one of the city's official house museums, is allowed to employ someone to watch over the building. In exchange for living in the cottage rent-free, Mr. Moakley is responsible for providing security, handling emergencies, and spending a day a week taking care of the house and its grounds. He vacuums. He dusts. He polishes the furniture, washes the windows, paints over scratches on the walls, and nails down errant floorboards. He sets out humane traps baited with peanut-butter sandwiches to catch the squirrels that make a mess of the attic.

Many people would conclude that having to preside over an old and demanding residence in a remote corner of the city with no one to turn to when the boiler croaks or a floorboard snaps loose represents the worst of all possible worlds. Even under the best of circumstances, the tasks might seem never-ending. "There's always something to be done," Mr. Moakley says. "Raking the leaves. Shoveling the snow. Getting the garden ready for planting. Planning the next exhibition. You can never lie on the couch and feel that everything is finished." Yet an advantage of coming from a family of construction workers is that even complicated maintenance tasks seem easy. "I'm not afraid of tools," he says. "In the house where I grew up, if something was broken, we'd all sit around and watch my father fix it."

Another issue is privacy. Sometimes Mr. Moakley finds a stranger standing in his living room, a visitor to the museum who took a wrong turn and accidentally wandered up the narrow staircase that leads to the second floor. And while the park surrounding the museum is officially closed at night, Mr. Moakley must sometimes shoo away rowdy teenagers carousing outside his windows, gently reminding them that he's trying to sleep.

You can't help wondering if he's lonely out here, in a setting someone once described as his Elysian sanctuary. At the same time, the upsides are considerable, a major one being that the apartment is eminently suitable for entertaining, thanks largely to a porch with a glorious view of the water. In Austen's day, the house was called Clear Comfort. Mr. Moakley's friends call it Camp Comfort and often arrive with bags of groceries, happy to hang out for the weekend and in good weather to dine alfresco. "We'll come to Camp Comfort, and you'll cook," they announce cheerfully to Mr. Moakley, and he does just that, sometimes whipping up Mediterranean dishes using recipes he learned from his days working as a waiter at an island restaurant called Aesop's Tables. "It's like having a little bed-and-breakfast," he says of the setup. "But I'm lucky it's so nice. I'm not sure people would come otherwise."

His work and his life are fully integrated. Although he seemed to have fallen into this berth almost accidentally, this place suits him. Living here also gives Mr. Moakley a chance to partake of a largely forgotten moment in the city's cultural history. Austen is intensely present, at least in spirit. She lived at Clear Comfort for more than half a century, much of the time with her longtime companion, Gertrude Amelia Tate, producing 9,000 glass-plate negatives, a third of which survive. But despite her impressive career and prodigious output, things ended badly. Toward the end of her life, she lost her house, was officially declared a pauper, and ended up in the poorhouse, from which she was rescued by friends just before her death.

Mr. Moakley hopes to one day compile a book of Austen's photographs. But if he does, he may not be able to pore over her haunting black-and-white images of a lost city on the site where so much of her creative life took place. Although his appointment as custodian of her cottage is open-ended, he realizes that his time here won't last forever. "As much as this is my home," Mr. Moakley explains, "I know that I'm just Austen's caretaker." When those days are over? "I'll most likely be living in an apartment like everyone else," he says. "Though I'll probably stay on Staten Island and watch the other guy rake the leaves."

# 10

# The Domestication of a Dive

## Joel Hinman and His Family in NoHo

**FEBRUARY 14, 2010**

Joel Hinman, a writer and filmmaker, and his family in a converted loft in NoHo. (Nicole Bengiveno/*The New York Times*)

THE 1970s and '80s are on thrilling and sometimes terrifying display in the fifth-floor apartment at 640 Broadway where Joel Hinman has lived for the past 35 years.

One of the two Beaux-Arts windows in the living room—eight-foot-wide half moons that stare like giant empty eyes onto the intersection of Broadway and Bleecker Street—is pocked with a semicircle of bullet holes. Mr. Hinman suspects that they date from the years the law commune that served the Black Panthers had its headquarters on this floor.

The dramas unspooled into the '90s. Long after Mr. Hinman's arrival as a raw 20-something from Connecticut, he used to gaze longingly at the orgies taking place in an apartment across the street. "The shades are up, there's hard-core porn on the TV, they're going at it, and you're feeling like you're never invited to the right parties," Mr. Hinman, a 57-year-old writer who has spent much of his career making concert films and other documentaries, recalls as he stands by that window and talks wistfully about the old days. "And I'm wondering: How can I ever get over there? Do I do the old 'Hi, I'm bringing the pizza' joke?"

Outside his apartment door, the creaky elevator and the rickety staircase that winds up nine stories bring to mind another defining aspect of those years, the nearly three decades that Martin Fine was the building's landlord. Even in an era in which slumlords seemed to rule the town, Mr. Fine was a legend in New York real estate circles. The building where Mr. Hinman lived was in such bad shape that for three years neither Con Ed nor the phone company would let their workers enter the basement; one winter, the place went without heat and elevator service for 80 days straight. Predictably, headline writers at the tabs had a field day with Fine and his transgressions; to them, he was the Ghoul of Gentrification, the King of Pain.

In 1995, the same year a workman died in the collapse of a Fine-owned building in Hell's Kitchen, the landlord found himself on the annual list of the city's 10 worst landlords compiled by the newspaper columnist Jack Newfield. Given Mr. Hinman's politics, not to mention his intimate connection with Fine's management style, it's no surprise that a T-shirt showing Newfield's list splashed across the front page of *The New York Post* is among his prized possessions.

The apartment is nowadays the setting for a far tidier existence. Mr. Hinman, who teaches fiction and poetry at the Writers Studio and volunteers at a South Bronx organization that does mediation and conflict resolution, lives here with Kari Thorstensen, his wife of five years, and the couple's year-old son, Cyrus John Henry. But the space, for which they pay $1,300 a month, is in many ways still very much a bachelor pad, bearing witness to a wild ride of a life, or at least the wild rides of other people. Mr. Hinman, a terrific storyteller, talks about the old days with such gusto, you can't help but feel that he misses those years more than he lets on.

His stories also make you ponder New Yorkers' ambivalent relationship with the city's grittier decades. Is it better to live among investment bankers, as we do now, or among junkies and Black Panthers, as many people did back then? It's tempting to romanticize the bright lights and bright nights and to block out the violence and misery that also defined those years. Settings like Mr. Hinman's apartment, where the scruffy past peeks out despite itself, makes it hard to avoid such questions.

Telling Mr. Hinman's story, however, involves going back to a far more distant era. The first Hinman arrived in Connecticut from England in 1650; in recounting his family's early history, Mr. Hinman likes to mention a namesake ancestor who fought in the Revolutionary War and so despised the British that when he received a fatal bullet in the leg, he demanded that the bullet be removed, lest he die with British lead in his body. But the family eventually made peace with their forebears. Mr. Hinman's sofa is heaped with needlepoint cushions stitched by his mother, a devout reader of *Majesty* magazine, that bear the royal British lion, along with the Hinman family crest.

By the 20th century, at least some of the Hinmans had become Brooklyn burghers, whose holdings included the Erie Basin, the venerable Brooklyn shipyard. The property was sold in 1953, the year Mr. Hinman was born, but a huge black-and-white photograph of the complex hangs in the hallway that winds through his apartment, a reminder of the era when *On the Waterfront* and *All My Sons* defined the part of Brooklyn where Ikea and Fairway now reign.

Mr. Hinman's building, a brown brick commercial structure built in 1897, had a solid if drab history; in its small industrial spaces, workers produced everything from towels to buttons to badges. But by 1975, when Mr. Hinman and a college friend arrived, both the building and the surrounding area were on the ropes. Heroin battered the streets, soon to be replaced by crack cocaine. The neighborhood, by then heavily Hispanic, had become a dumping ground for methadone addicts and homeless women, its liquor stores patronized by dozy men in pursuit of their pint bottles.

Inside 640 Broadway, the remaining factories were interspersed with a few hardy residential tenants, Mr. Hinman and his roommate among them. "A guy named Sally, a guy with a big pompadour, ran the elevator," he says. "My college buddy and I were both 21. We were completely clueless about what we were getting into." The premises left much to be desired, but at $500 for 2,500 square feet, the rent seemed awfully cheap. "We thought we were sharp operators," he says. "In our dreams."

For most of the past 35 years, Mr. Hinman occupied the apartment without a lease. The setup wasn't exactly legal, but there wasn't a dull moment. In the apartment at the rear of the floor, which was reached only through Mr. Hinman's quarters, the residents lived especially large. He remembers experiments with angel dust, screenings of human dismemberment films from Peru, and the night five guys showed up dressed up as Arab women. "I thought I was some radical dude, seeing all that," Mr. Hinman says almost proudly. Cops from what he describes as the violent predators squad arrived with regularity. As the party raged on, the building sank ever deeper into decay.

In his apartment, the kitchen sink fell through the counter, and mushrooms sprouted in the carpet under the bed. Over a two-week period, he killed nine rats, clubbing one unfortunate victim to death in a scene so vicious Mr. Hinman compares it to the last 15 minutes of *Jaws*. He shocked others into unconsciousness, then drowned them in tubs of water. In a folder somewhere, he has photographs.

Over the years, friends crashed and roommates drifted in and out, leaving behind an ever-expanding collection of junk. Broken television sets. A trouser press. ("God knows why.") Someone's wedding dress. Mr. Hinman thinks the owner's name was Bonnie. Yet despite the chaos, there were reasons to stay. "I had this fabulous huge place with cheap rent and great architecture," he says. "I could have lots of roommates to reduce the cost." Given all the space, he could run his production company out of the back room and live in the front. The neighborhood, too, offered endless diversion. Two years before he arrived, the punk-rock palace known as CBGB's had opened a couple of blocks away, and its glitter spilled out onto the street. Plus he was young; especially back then, that explained a lot.

Today most of the odder items are gone from these rooms, and concessions have been made to the apartment's newer occupants. Cyrus occupies a pastel nursery with a domed ceiling. Ms. Thorstensen, a technology product management consultant, works in a tasteful gray office. In the kitchen, magnetized spice jars cling to a wall like shiny barnacles, and the cabinet doors have no handles, a design detail that gives them a sleek, minimalist look. Metal lanterns from Anthropologie, an unexpected touch of high-fashion décor, dangle on either side of those great windows, which are framed by palm trees and edged with pots of geraniums, rosemary, aloe, and papyrus plants.

Yet even now, with a wife, baby, and a 200-pound Saint Bernard in residence, remnants of the old days endure. The ancient butler's table looks as if it has witnessed a million parties. So does the beat-up leather sofa, so huge that when Mr. Hinman wanted it re-covered, the upholsterers had to make a house call. Jagged strips of decorative copper trim, its edges sharp as fangs, snake around one wall. "The place was in such bad shape that the guy who came to child-proof the apartment before Cyrus was born showed up a month early," Mr. Hinman says. "And after he looked around, he said it was the second-worst place he had ever seen."

# 11

# A Man and His Miscellany

John Foxell on Staten Island

MARCH 19, 2010

John Foxell, a writer, folk artist, and self-described eccentric, in his 19th-century saltbox on Staten Island. (Paul Moakley for *The New York Times*)

P ASSERS-BY invariably slow down in front of the 19th-century salt-box-style house on Cottage Place where John Foxell has lived for a quarter of a century, and for good reason. The pumpkin clapboard edged with jet-black trim is a tip of the hat to the days when Cottage Place, near the north shore of Staten Island, was known as Halloween Street. Two signs outside pay tribute to the legendary social activist Dorothy Day, whom Mr. Foxell came to know in the '60s during his days as a young conscientious objector.

The cottage is also framed by two quirky wood-frame buildings. The one Mr. Foxell calls a prayer house is wreathed with stained glass, topped with a cross, and bears a quotation from Gandhi. The one he calls a spirit house also features stained glass, but the quotation is from Horace. On Sundays, Mr. Foxell puts on a special tie and sits inside the prayer house, reading a book or one of his many copies of the Bible. At night, he some-times sits in the spirit house and looks at the moon.

Outside the cottage hangs a blanket bearing an image of Our Lady of Guadalupe, and on occasion, one of the many Mexican immigrants who have settled in this community will kneel on the sidewalk and pray. "Is this a church?" they sometimes wonder aloud. "Maybe a museum?" No, Mr. Foxell replies gently. It's a private home. "I don't know what to tell people," he says. "I just choose to live differently."

Differently is an understatement. In this idiosyncratic cottage, which appears to have wandered onto the island by way of a Grimms' fairy tale, this erudite 65-year-old artist, writer, and self-confessed eccentric has surrounded himself with a vast collection of sculptures and artifacts from around the world (though acquired largely from antique shops closer to home). Many of them are poignant, some are unsettling, and a few are ghoulish.

But what's most remarkable about Mr. Foxell is that he lives a life largely untouched by modern technology. He doesn't use computers. He hasn't driven a car for more than 20 years. He has no television set, and though he owns 10 vintage radios, he never turns them on. (He does have a cell phone, but one suspects that he uses it less than most people.) He has never had a credit card or a checking account; he pays cash for every purchase, even this house. In his entire life, he has never sent an e-mail; instead, he writes letters, in the spiky handwriting his father taught him

60 years ago. Every morning he walks to the local library and reads a paper copy of *The New York Times.*

Mr. Foxell's explanation for his avoidance of so much of modern-day technology is simple: "I've tried not to participate in the world I see," he explains. "I insulate myself."

In person, Mr. Foxell cuts an imposing, if somewhat otherworldly, figure. His longish dark hair, his strong handshake, his slow baritone, and the thick, steel-rimmed glasses without which he is nearly blind combine to give him a powerful presence. It is, however, his self-imposed isolation from the thrum and static of modern life that makes him seem so unusual and makes a visit to his house feel like a pilgrimage to another time, perhaps a better time. He lives a life that feels remarkable in the early 21st century, his days and nights free of incessant electronic chatter, free of screens, beeps, and nonstop being in touch. It's not that he lives off the grid exactly but that he seems to live on a grid of his own making. All this helps explain why certain people find Mr. Foxell's story moving, even inspiring. He lives according to values that seem in increasingly short supply in this postmillennium metropolis.

Mr. Foxell may be eccentric and something of a Luddite, but no one would describe him as a recluse. Wearing the identical outfit every day, a black corduroy suit and heavy black oxfords, he attends plays, concerts, movies, art exhibitions, and parties. Up at 6, late to bed (he sleeps only a few hours a night), he writes fiction and has built hundreds of whimsical folk-art-like constructions made of found objects, like the one titled *Five Minutes to Midnight*, which features a ticking watch and a plastic statuette of Jesus Christ. Mr. Foxell has also read every one of the 6,000 books arranged alphabetically on the floor-to-ceiling shelves that line his living room walls. "Reading is my life," he says. "My friends were always in books." A bit improbably, he goes on cruises.

The circuitous journey that brought Mr. Foxell to this house began in 1952 when his family moved to Staten Island, the closest thing his parents could find to Troy, the city in upstate New York where he was born and spent his early years. After graduating from New York University, Mr. Foxell bounced around the United States and Canada and changed his name frequently, largely to avoid the Vietnam draft. Over 44 years, he held 29 jobs, everything from button-factory worker to census taker. An alcoholic for a decade, he inhabited many a Skid Row before taking his final drink 34 years ago.

By the early 1980s, Mr. Foxell was back in Staten Island, yearning for a more settled life. In 1984, on a Friday the 13th that would have struck a more traditional individual as inauspicious, he saw the house on Cottage Place and bought it instantly for $40,000.

The two-story building, which is festooned with a porch and a peaked roof, had sat on this site at least since 1848 and was in abysmal condition by the time Mr. Foxell arrived. The carpets were threadbare and the walls so spongy you could poke a finger through them. Ceilings hidden by acoustic tiles sagged halfway to the floor. Over the years, Mr. Foxell spent upward of $400,000 to restore the shell and to imprint these chilly, pleasantly musty rooms with his singular taste. Every door and window was replaced with stained glass, acquired from 29 different churches around the metropolitan area; it's no wonder strangers wonder if this is a place of worship. To "cathedralize" the ceilings, he knocked out the attic. Today, nearly every room has an embossed tin ceiling, each with a different pattern. Mr. Foxell also installed air-conditioning and a burglar alarm, "which is," he says drily, "about as much as I'm willing to adapt to modern times."

The décor, if that's not too highfalutin a word for what some might consider an inspired mishmash, includes such artworks and collectibles from Africa and Asia as elephant tusks, voodoo dolls, and masks that gaze balefully at visitors. The house is also rich in ecclesiastical items, among them a church pew, a font for holy water, and an assortment of crucifixes, because, their owner says, "you can never have too many crucifixes." Although Mr. Foxell isn't Jewish, his religious possessions include a shofar, which his friend Rabbi Sussman blows on Rosh Hashanah, along with a menorah, a mezuzah, and a skull bearing the Star of David. "A reminder of the Holocaust," Mr. Foxell says. "Even if it's difficult, these things keep you from forgetting too much."

From his childhood home come his parents' bed, on which he was conceived, along with his mother's hope chest and an army of faded family photographs. One from 1969 shows a long-haired Mr. Foxell at Woodstock, where he handed out lemons filled with LSD-laced cottage cheese. In the snug back parlor hangs a letter from Eleanor Roosevelt, whom Mr. Foxell interviewed for his high school paper, along with a photograph of a young John Foxell standing next to President Truman. Upon learning that the former president was in town and receiving the press at the Carlyle Hotel every morning at 6:20, the student from Staten Island showed up, announced to an aide, "I'm the press," and was rewarded for his efforts with a comment on Jackie Kennedy's miniskirts that was picked up by the wire services. "He was one of my five favorite presidents," Mr. Foxell said. "Except, of course, for the atom bomb."

Many of Mr. Foxell's possessions might strike a more squeamish individual as uncommonly grisly, among them the necklace made of human bones, the box containing a sad handful of children's teeth, hollow-eyed skulls that peer gloomily from corners, and especially the open coffins on either side of the guest bed that contain full-body skeletons. Wandering these rooms, it's hard not to wonder how a person can live a tranquil life in such a setting. Yet these memento mori do not offend him. On the contrary, objects that most people would find unsettling bring him comfort, even solace. "They remind us that we're just a stack of bones, that we're just passing through," Mr. Foxell says. They also remind him that people rarely go gentle into that good night. "We shouldn't pretend that death is fun and games until the last minute," he says.

The oddities extend to the kitchen, home to a 1934 ball-top General Electric refrigerator containing only grapefruit juice and yogurt. A small cabinet filled entirely with bottles of pills testifies to the fact that Mr. Foxell has, in many respects, led a hard life. The pantry is stocked with cans bearing the label "Creamed possum"—a gag item but one that seems oddly at home here. "Survival food," Mr. Foxell says with a trace of a smile.

Until a few years ago, Mr. Foxell worked in the office of family court judge Judith Sheindlin—"when she was a real judge," as he describes the jurist who became far more celebrated as television's Judge Judy. Today he lives on his pension and Social Security, and in no way does he rue his deeply checkered past. "I'm glad I'm me," he says. "For a writer, a troubled history gives you a lot to draw on."

# 12

# A Beach Bungalow with a Magnetic Pull

## Susan Anderson in Far Rockaway, Queens

OCTOBER 24, 2010

Susan Anderson, an artist, in her restored bungalow in Far Rockaway, Queens. (Christian Hansen for *The New York Times*)

I F ever an image captured the rhythms of summer for generations of working-class New Yorkers, it was the humble Rockaway bungalow.

By the early '30s, more than 7,000 of these Hansel-and-Gretel-like cottages lined the 11-mile-long Queens peninsula, their very silhouettes evoking nostalgia-soaked memories. In these little houses with their peaked roofs and diminutive proportions, generations of New Yorkers, many from immigrant backgrounds, celebrated the season. The buildings themselves functioned almost as madeleines, evoking memories of white-uniformed ice cream salesmen trolling the sands, sweaty encounters under the boardwalk, and the jangly sounds of honky-tonk amusements. Even allowing for the softening glaze of memory, these summers were often idyllic interludes in intensely urban lives, a too-brief respite from stuffy apartments on treeless streets.

Like so many remnants of an earlier New York, the bungalows of the Rockaways are vanishing. The postwar era brought high-rises and an influx of poor and minority residents to the peninsula. Today, perhaps fewer than 400 bungalows remain, the rest lost to development or neglect. But if a single survivor embodies the spirit of its predecessors, it's the bungalow at the foot of Beach 26th Street in Far Rockaway, home for the past three years to an artist and woman of all trades named Susan Anderson. Exquisitely restored, studded with unusual found objects and glowing with an unearthly light, this house seems a throwback to an era disappearing in the rearview mirror.

Ms. Anderson grew up in Arizona and came to New York as a college student in the early 1980s aboard the Green Tortoise, a vehicle that featured beds but no seats. Once arrived, she bounced from one odd job to another, the oddest being her stint as O. J. Sue, for which she sold freshly squeezed orange juice on Wall Street from a retrofitted wheelchair turned food truck. She also bounced from apartment to apartment. Yet wherever she lived, the bungalows of the Rockaways exerted a mystical pull.

Accompanied by a group of friends, Ms. Anderson made her first visit to the Rockaways in 1984, when she was living in a loft in Park Slope, Brooklyn, and found herself entranced by a cluster of white stucco bungalows, each being advertised for $30,000. As she and her friends wandered onto their porches, she was reminded of ancient villages she had seen on her travels. "They looked like a stage set," she says, "or a lost world waiting to be repopulated." Had she ventured deeper into the neighborhood, however, she would have seen streets pockmarked with burned-out buildings and a community, devastated by AIDS and wracked by crime, drugs, and wrenching poverty, that felt deeply forbidding.

In 1999, ensconced in another Park Slope loft, Ms. Anderson made a return visit, traveling out on her bike to see what had become of the area that had intrigued her 15 years earlier. "And in a weird way," she says, "it was as if the world had stood still. The water was pristine. Even though it was summer, there was nobody on the beach." A boarded-up bungalow being offered at the bargain-basement price of $15,000 looked tempting, despite the absence of part of the roof and the façade. By the time she got around to making an offer, however, she was moments too late. The bungalow had just been sold.

Her third visit, again on her bike, occurred in the summer of 2002, but an effort to buy a bungalow advertised for $20,000 fell through because of missed communications with the real estate agent handling the sale. Nor was the neighborhood much improved; this might have been the visit during which a cop cautioned ominously, "Honey, you don't want to live here."

On a summer day in 2003, by then living in the East Village, Ms. Anderson returned a fourth time. A homeless man who lived in a van on a grassy field—a muscular guy wearing a wife-beater, a doo-rag, and tattoos—directed her attention to a bungalow on the lot next door. Two pit bulls were chained to the front porch, which was wrapped in rusty chicken wire. Cardboard covered the portion of the old front door once graced by glass, and a piece of rotting wood was attached to the gate.

Not until a frigid evening later that year did Ms. Anderson get a chance to inspect the interior. "It was an awful night," she recalls. "The Hudson was frozen. The field was frozen. And, my God, the house was a hellhole!" Because the bathroom had no floor, you could see down to the dirt. Squatters had invaded the interior, leaving as calling cards their trademark graffiti. The wind, a killer because of the closeness of the water, howled through thin walls whose holes had been patched with scraps of plywood in a half-hearted effort to keep out the elements. Although Ms. Anderson didn't notice it at the time, the streets were so littered with drug paraphernalia that locals called the area Crack Alley. She would eventually discover used syringes and other instruments of a quick fix buried in the ground like grim exotic plants.

Yet despite the bungalow's dilapidated state, Ms. Anderson was drawn by its possibilities. The following November, she and a friend bought the house, along with a sister cottage to the rear, for $120,000. Two years ago, when the friend decided that she wasn't cut out for bungalow life, Ms. Anderson's brother bought out her share, and today Ms. Anderson uses the second cottage as a studio.

Few people would have had the physical and emotional stamina to take on the task of rescuing so troubled a structure or the flair to transform what many would consider a ruin. But Ms. Anderson used to do construction work to help support her career as an artist, and in restoring a building that dated to around 1920, her skills served her well. With the help of professionals but doing much of the heavy lifting herself, she repaired the roof, installed a heating unit, ripped away linoleum to expose the pine floors, and opened the warren of tiny rooms to create a tapestry of larger, airier spaces. The dropped ceiling was torn out to reveal the attic, topped with the original cedar shakes and crisscrossed with the old beams. During the early stages of renovation, Ms. Anderson sometimes slept up there, swaddled in a down jacket to keep warm.

Not until three years after she bought the bungalow was it suitable for full-time occupancy, and despite her considerable sweat equity, she sunk $100,000 into renovations. But the experience transformed her into a fierce partisan of bungalow life, deeply appreciative of these cottages' quirky charms and passionate about rescuing those that remain while there's time.

"This house turned out a hundred times better than I thought it would," Ms. Anderson says. "There's something wonderfully beautiful about the architecture. There's not a lot of unnecessary gesture." Fittingly, she enjoys a star turn in *The Bungalows of Rockaway*, a new documentary by Jennifer Callahan; she's the small, brown-haired woman seen watering a rainbow assortment of flowers during a montage of images of bungalow life.

The most remarkable aspect of the house is the light. Ms. Anderson has covered the 11 small windows with sheets of waxed paper, and the result is a soft glow, as if the rooms are illuminated from within. The addition of a few interior windows, along with votive candles and lighting fixtures made of paper, fabric, and crystals, contributes to the otherworldly mood.

The deftness with which Ms. Anderson has preserved the building's bones is equally impressive; in those bones you can trace the bungalow's entire history. She has exposed many of the original beams and lathing, and much of the plaster over the lathing, to create abstract decorative effects. Remnants of old wallpaper bearing faint images of sheep and cabbage roses cling to the walls, a ghostly reminder of families who inhabited these rooms decades earlier. Thanks to graceful arrangements of reeds, dried hydrangeas, and beach grass, along with scraps of wood salvaged from the boardwalk, the border between the inside and outside world seems porous. That's by design. "The goal," Ms. Anderson says, "was to bring the bungalow back to itself."

The house is sparsely furnished, dotted with small, old-fashioned chairs and other castoffs. The bare-bones kitchen is stocked with minimal provisions—cereal, cookies, pasta, coffee. Odds and ends from the streets sit on a shelf, among them a perfectly preserved dragonfly, a pair of cobalt-blue dominoes, cloudy milk bottles bearing the word "Borden," and a lone green plastic soldier, separated for eternity from his brother warriors.

In Ms. Anderson's workroom, doll-size suitcases are arranged in a pile. You wonder if they're a plaything for her cat, Moses, an enchanting creature with silky black fur and gemlike green eyes. But no. This is where Ms. Anderson eats dinner.

Regardless of the season, Ms. Anderson can smell the ocean and hear the pounding of the waves. During a cloudburst, rain pelts her walls so violently that she feels as if she's in the heart of the storm, being tossed about in her little house like Dorothy in *The Wizard of Oz*.

It goes without saying that such a spartan, stripped-down existence is hardly for everyone. Some people might go quietly mad in such a place, here near the next-to-the-last stop on the subway, so close to the end of the line that the train is practically empty by the time it reaches her station. At the very least, a person might be desperately lonely. But Ms. Anderson is made of sturdy stuff. She has her work, creating sliverlike paintings that she describes as "slices of the real world." She has her cat, along with escape hatches in the form of keys to the apartments of three friends in Manhattan. Perhaps most important, she has the temperament and ability to forge a life for herself in a setting others might find daunting beyond words, although she'd be the first to admit that doing so has involved considerable struggle.

Also, she's not quite alone. "I see squirrels running around, and rabbits," she says. "I saw a possum outside my window, and one night I heard an unearthly sound on the roof that turned out to be a raccoon." Seagulls and egrets squawk on her porch, and piping plovers nest nearby.

For all she senses the presence of the city, she could be on a windswept beach in Maine. And especially in winter, when the wind howls and the thunder crashes, she feels protected from the elements, embraced by her four small walls. "Plus there's a certain survival thing that goes on out here," she says. "It's definitely been real. I mean knife-on-your-skin real."

# 13

# The Almost Landless Gardener

## Catherine Fitzsimons in Brooklyn Heights

FEBRUARY 25, 2011

Cathy Fitzsimons, a landscape designer, in her 19th-century home in Brooklyn Heights. (Donna Alberico for *The New York Times*)

THE cobblestone blocks of Joralemon Street are one of the loveliest parts of Brooklyn Heights. Come spring, and into the fall, the front gardens of the multimillion-dollar brownstones that line this stretch will be lush with greenery, and their window boxes will explode with flowers. But even on this beautiful strip, the low-slung red-brick building just off Hicks Street stands out.

Catherine Fitzsimons, who has lived here for three decades, is a landscape designer who specializes in what she diplomatically calls "city-sized" gardens, and throughout much of the year, her narrow front yard is filled with small trees and pots of flowering shrubs waiting to be delivered to clients. In spring, Ms. Fitzsimons's neighbors stop to admire the brilliant gold forsythia and the profusion of rosy azaleas and rhododendrons. In summer, they pause in front of the hydrangeas and butterfly bushes and sniff a fragrant shrub called summersweet. Even in winter, the yard tempts the eye with pots of witch hazel and pussywillow.

Passers-by who stop to admire the profusion of flowers and greenery invariably check to see if Aurora, Ms. Fitzsimons's fluffy gold and white cat, is nestled under a chair. Aurora is not only beautiful; she's also sweet-natured, so sociable that she practically smiles at people surveying the offerings of the day.

"She's a very lovey-dovey cat," Ms. Fitzsimons says on a gray, tag-end-of-winter morning as the object of her words sits placidly on her lap. "She's not standoffish at all. I think she likes the admiration." Because Aurora came from a shelter, her origins are mysterious, but Ms. Fitzsimons thinks that she must be a Maine Coon because she looks exactly like the photograph of a Maine Coon on the calendar on her refrigerator.

Ms. Fitzsimons and Aurora occupy most of a two-story structure that's attached to the town house on the corner and that probably began life as a shed or a garage. Ms. Fitzsimons, who was born and raised in Hamden, Connecticut, arrived in 1980 as a 20-something renter, and five years later, when the apartment went co-op, she bought it for under $60,000. The apartment is also the headquarters of her landscape design firm, Willowtown Gardens, which she runs with her sister and whose work can be seen throughout the neighborhood.

Even in Brooklyn Heights, which sometimes feels pleasantly frozen in another era, Ms. Fitzsimons's house is redolent with a sense of the past. The first floor, which is mostly living room, is just 11 feet by 17 feet. A narrow winding staircase leads to an even more diminutive bedroom. There are no perfect right angles. The floors are pine, the walls white brick. From the street, copper pots are visible through the filmy white curtains in the front window. With its modest proportions, small upper-story windows, wooden beams atop eight-foot plaster ceilings, and ancient radiators and steam pipes, the little house seems like a cozy, if sometimes chilly, relic from the 19th century even though constucted in the early 20th century.

"There's not a lot of insulation," admits Ms. Fitzsimons, who has done a considerable amount of work on the house, much of it with her own hands. A few years ago, she tore down the first-floor ceiling, parts of which were collapsing, and installed insulation between the beams. She suspects she may never complete all the tasks she has in mind.

Practically nothing in the house is new. "A hundred percent gifts and finds" is how Ms. Fitzsimons describes the furnishings, right down to the mismatched flowered china and Waterford wine goblets in the glass-paned cupboards. Nevertheless, her possessions speak to a family history that goes back several generations, starting with an elaborately crafted French clock, circa 1800, that came mysteriously to Ms. Fitzsimons's grandfather.

"This is the real thing," she says, carefully taking the small bronze clock down from a shelf. Its centerpiece is a handsome young Roman holding a book in one hand and surrounded by the classical symbols of learning—a globe, a protractor, the lamp of knowledge. "Who the heck knows where my grandfather got it," she says. "He wasn't a big collector. But it's fancy-schmancy, no?"

Fancy-schmancy indeed. The clock, which was made by hand, operates with what's known as a silk-thread suspension mechanism, an ingenious device in which the pendulum hangs from a tiny loop of silk thread. To Ms. Fitzsimons's dismay, this mechanism is quite temperamental. "I've spent $800 getting it fixed, but it didn't stay fixed," she says. She wants the clock to work so she can hear the delicate ping of the chimes, but for now the project is on hold.

Near the clock stands a framed photograph of Ms. Fitzsimons's father, Daniel Edward Fitzsimons, who owned an insurance company in New Haven and who died in 1970, when his daughter, one of five children, was 16. "What I like about this picture," she says, "is that it shows my dad as a young man, when he was just starting out in the world," and in fact this clean-cut, serious-looking individual seems to personify the optimistic face of the 1950s, the period in which this photograph was taken. Ms. Fitzsimons also has a 1915 diploma from the Butler School of Business in New Haven that was awarded to her namesake great-aunt, a document proclaiming that the school "cheerfully recommends her to the favor of the business community."

The small white settee in the living room was created using the frame of a narrow twin bed, "because in a room like this, you need petite." The settee is covered with a quilt made by Ms. Fitzsimons's mother, Barbara, described by her daughter as a demon quilter, even at the age of 83. The ladder chairs with the woven rush seats came from her great-aunts Catherine and Anna. Linens are stored in a bird's-eye maple secretary that she found on the street.

Perhaps unsurprisingly for a woman whose career involves bringing beauty and environmental health to this and other neighborhoods, Ms. Fitzsimons is one of those New Yorkers who has devoted an enormous amount of unpaid time and energy opposing projects that could harm the community and championing those that would be beneficial. Thanks partly to her efforts, the cobblestone portion of Joralemon Street was runner-up two years in a row for the honor of being anointed greenest block in Brooklyn. (Locals hoped that a $900 investment in geraniums and oak-leaf hydrangeas would help them snag first place, but their dreams were dashed.) When plans for a Brooklyn Bridge Park on steroids were unveiled a decade ago, Ms. Fitzsimons was the first of her neighbors to hang a flag bearing the Revolutionary War motto "Don't Tread on Me" from her window.

The campaign closest to her heart was the one on behalf of Van Voorhees Park, a public park and playground in neighboring Cobble Hill, part of which was proposed as the site of a hospital parking garage. On one wall hangs a scroll honoring the struggle, ultimately unsuccessful, to keep out the garage, from a group called Friends of Shinobazu Pond, a sacred lotus pond in Tokyo that was similarly threatened. "It was a hard-fought effort," Ms. Fitzsimons says, recalling with mixed emotions the drama of that battle. "We really went bananas there for a few years in the early '90s."

Much of her work on behalf of the park was conducted at the small white desk in a corner of the upstairs bedroom. The desk also functions as what Ms. Fitzsimons describes as the command center for her business, which takes its name from the old name of this section of Brooklyn Heights. A quarter-century-old Rolodex holds all her contact information.

Most of the rest of the space in this room is occupied by a large maple bed, a gift from her great-aunt Catherine and topped with a quilt that her mother sewed from scraps of a green, pink, and turquoise Lilly Pulitzer dress that Ms. Fitzsimons wore in college. Aurora can often be found plopped on top of the quilt, gazing through the tall windows at the gardens behind the house and especially at the trees—the weeping willow, the white dogwood, the pink magnolia, the red maple, the pale pink weeping cherry. Ms. Fitzsimons loves them too. Even in winter, when the branches are bare, she can see their colors in her mind's eye.

In cold weather, Aurora sometimes sits on the shelf above the radiator—"the warmest spot in the house," according to her mistress—watching as squirrels dart about the branches. Aurora is the most peaceable of creatures, but one suspects that in eyeing the squirrels she's contemplating what she hopes will be her next meal.

# 14

# Lair and Sanctuary in the South Bronx

## Carol Zakaluk and John Knoerr in Mott Haven, the Bronx

**MARCH 18, 2011**

Carol Zakaluk and John Knoerr in her family's row house in Mott Haven in the Bronx. (Suzanne DeChillo/*The New York Times*)

CAROL ZAKALUK lives on what's known as the Bertine block in the Mott Haven section of the South Bronx, a stretch of ruddy brick and stone row houses built in the 1890s. The strip takes its name from the local developer, George Bertine, but the buildings themselves were the work of a single gifted architect named George Keister. The house at 422 East 136th Street, which Ms. Zakaluk occupies with her husband, John Knoerr, has been in her family for 90 years. And by stepping outside her front door, she can retrace the geography of her childhood.

The building next door at No. 420, which she bought at a discount from her parents and now rents to a revolving group of young tenants, is the one in which she was born and raised. "Here's where my crib was," Ms. Zakaluk says, pointing to a corner of the dining room. "And here's where there used to be the round oak table where I did my homework, under a yellow lamp that hung from the ceiling."

The garden-level kitchen also evokes razor-sharp recollections, as if through muscle memory she can retrieve fragments of her past. "When I bend down to collect the recyclables," she says, "I remember, almost without thinking about it, the kittens who used to live under the staircase."

Across the street stood the apartment house where Ms. Zakaluk's paternal grandfather, a grocer from the Ukraine named Michael Zakaluk, lived with his wife, Anastasia. The house where Ms. Zakaluk and her husband live had been bought in 1921 for $7,800 by her maternal grandfather, Karel Boekhoff, a Dutch upholsterer. When he and his wife, Harriet, moved in, their daughter, Clara, who would grow up to become Carol's mother, was 3. A formal family portrait taken around that time shows a dark-eyed man with a mustache, a woman holding a baby in a long white christening dress—that was baby Mary—and Clara, a huge bow in her hair, perched on her father's knee. Everyone looks deadly serious.

The story of 422 East 136th Street, one that spans four generations and involves a sprawling cast of characters, is complex. But the tale is also rich, encompassing both architectural distinction and the experiences of a large and close-knit family that, unlike the vast majority of its neighbors, rode out the turmoil that convulsed this section of the Bronx in the later 20th century. At the heart of the story stands the four-story, single-family house that Mr. Boekhoff bought so many decades ago, one of 10 Queen Anne–style structures whose façades are encrusted with stained glass and ornamental wrought iron and whose low stoops and tall chimneys add an air of domesticity. The strip was built at a moment Mott Haven was a destination for middle-class families seeking a fashionable neighborhood, and the variety of rooftops—rounded, square, peaked, stepped—gives the impression that the architect was showing off.

Today, the exterior of No. 422 looks much as it did a century earlier. Irises that Ms. Zakaluk's grandmother planted still come up every spring in the back garden, near the swing set her grandfather built from old plumbing parts. By 1984, Ms. Zakaluk was living on the top floor with Mr. Knoerr and her daughter, and she acquired the house after the death of her grandmother the following year.

And despite the presence of two busy professionals in their 50s—Mr. Knoerr is a sound engineer, and Ms. Zakaluk has had various careers in the arts, including book designer and sculptor's assistant—the interior is little changed as well. Only three items of furniture aren't indigenous to the house or to Ms. Zakaluk's family. "If it's not broken, don't throw it away—that was our family's mantra," Ms. Zakaluk says. "We were recyclers before they had the word." Because her mother's mother was one of 10 siblings, all of whom lived in New York, there was much to be handed down from one generation to the next. Even the kitchen, the only room that has seen any renovation to speak of, is as vintage as they come. "In 2008, I finally sold the old Vulcan gas stove, which dated from 1921 or maybe even earlier, and the old GE refrigerator that my grandparents had used and that was at least 50 years old," Ms. Zakaluk says. But the original sink is still in place, along with the old cabinets and countertops and her great-aunt Elsie's metal kitchen table.

"And the dining room looks exactly the way it did when my grandparents lived here," she says. A chandelier edged with black and gold fringe that was original to the house illuminates her grandmother's dining room table. Dark wallpaper that resembles walnut paneling covers the walls, which are bordered with Dutch shelves, a term you rarely hear these days.

Also original to the house is the carved oak staircase, a gingerbread-like concoction of spindles and newel posts supporting a banister worn smooth by generations of hands. The front room too stands as a time capsule. When the Boekhoffs' son Robert died in 1940 at the age of 15, his wake was held in this space, which was redolent with the smell of flowers and the wax of melting candles. An ancient black trunk holds

150 letters that Ms. Zakaluk's parents wrote to each other during the Second World War. An ice chest that traveled to innumerable family picnics is stuffed with children's records bearing fetching names like "Peter, Please, It's Pancakes" to which Ms. Zakaluk sang along as a little girl. "Those were the principal things I did as a child," she says: "listen to records, read books, and play with the family kittens."

For much of the time that Ms. Zakaluk's family lived on the block, Mott Haven was a stable, if hardly affluent, neighborhood. St. Jerome's, the imposing Catholic church on East 138th Street, served as an anchor and source of stability. And when Ms. Zakaluk pictures her childhood, she sees the streets as they were more than half a century earlier. "I don't see the projects," she says of the 11 clusters of public housing that sprouted here after the war. "I see the buildings as they looked when I was 5—the five-story row houses, the charming candy store, the Irish bars, the remnants of the Third Avenue El."

Starting in the '60s, the world defined by these talismans came under siege as this part of the city was buffeted by social and economic havoc. "First there was heroin, then crack," Ms. Zakaluk recalls. "People were passed out on the streets. Brook Avenue and 139th Street was the crossroads of the drug trade, and the violence was in your face—you'd hear gunshots all the time." On the other side of her grandmother's house stood a drug house, "and every 15 minutes there would be a sale." At No. 422, all but one skylight was closed up when addicts took to racing across the roof, and masking tape still covers the hole in the blue, pink, and yellow stained-glass window, a relic from the night a drunken neighbor sent a bullet flying into the front room.

Almost miraculously, Ms. Zakaluk and her family escaped serious harm during those years. "There were so many people who knew our family, we were sort of immune," she explains. "When my mother went out, the guys on the street would say, 'Leave her alone, man, she lives here.'" Still, she remembers how she felt each time she walked out of her house, a shy young girl with blond hair as fine as spun sugar, sidestepping a knot of menacing-looking young men.

No one would have blamed her family had they left, and they themselves debated the issue seriously at least twice a year. "To stay or to go, that was the recurrent conversation around the dining room table," Ms. Zakaluk says. "But my parents had responsibility for their parents. If my parents left, they would have had to move three families." That her parents both taught at a local school was another incentive to stay. And an additional factor was at work. "We were a strong family," Ms. Zakaluk says. "And our sense of our house has always been as lair and sanctuary. When we came through the front door and locked the door behind us, we'd feel safe." Only once was that sense of safety violated, the time intruders broke in, and even then, no one was harmed.

Because the story of the devastation of the South Bronx is so familiar and because the city has been so transformed in recent decades, it's hard to remember how much areas like Mott Haven suffered in the latter part of the 20th century. It's hard to remember that these neighborhoods were so starved of basic human services—heat, water, decent schools and hospitals, and most of all the ability to come and go safely—they were routinely compared to parts of war-ravaged Europe. It's impossible not to admire the grit and stamina of families like the Zakaluks who stuck it out.

Just as the Zakaluks survived, so did the Bertine block, which escaped the worst of the horrors. Its beautiful row houses weren't laid waste by arson, one of the scourges of those years. The population, until recently black and Puerto Rican, is heavily Mexican. Ms. Zakaluk likes the diversity while also being glad that the neighborhood has managed to escape the gentrification lapping at the borough's southern tip.

Both Ms. Zakaluk's parents are dead, her mother in 2007 at 90, her father last March at 91. Yet they and their world are rarely far from her thoughts. "I talk to my parents periodically," Ms. Zakaluk admits. "They're my ghosts, and I'm happy to have them. And I'm very grateful to my grandparents for finding and keeping this place for so long."

# Creative Types

# 15

# The Traveling Circus Stops Here

## Seth Bloom and Christina Gelsone in West Harlem

JULY 5, 2009

Seth Bloom and Christina Gelsone, professional clowns, in their renovated railroad apartment in West Harlem. (Ruby Washington/*The New York Times*)

CHRISTINA GELSONE, a slender 36-year-old with delicate features and hair the color of a ripe eggplant, lies on her back on the bare parquet floor of her West Harlem apartment, an expectant look on her heart-shaped face. Her 34-year-old husband, whose dark hair shimmers with electric-blue highlights, stands over her, their palms touching. Then he swoops down until his body is balanced above hers, almost as if he is floating in the air. The couple hold the pose silently, the only sound on this quiet weekday afternoon the bird song outside their kitchen window and the rustle of leaves from nearby St. Nicholas Park.

Ms. Gelsone and Mr. Bloom are professional clowns, and they regularly perform feats like these in their fifth-floor walk-up in a small, turn-of-the-century apartment building on St. Nicholas Terrace. The onetime railroad flat is not only their home; it's also their rehearsal space and office, and a small room off the narrow hallway is crammed with such tools of their trade as stilts, water bombs, juggling pins, soap-bubble solution, and oversize balloons—not the items stashed in your average New York linen closet.

But Ms. Gelsone and Mr. Bloom, known professionally as the Acrobuffos, are hardly your average clowns. They perform their acrobatics, mime, juggling, and theatrics (but no fire-eating, Ms. Gelsone says, because it destroys your teeth) in some of the most troubled places on earth. They make annual visits to Afghanistan, where they met in the summer of 2003. They know it sounds like the start of a joke: "Two clowns meet in Afghanistan. . . ." Individually or as a pair they have also charmed crowds in Kosovo and Serbia in the Balkans, where memories of past conflicts are still raw.

"We're sometimes the only Americans without guns that people have seen in these places," Ms. Gelsone says after scrambling up from the floor and curling up next to her husband beside the wooden coffee table (at $350, one of the priciest items in the apartment). "You're just a little clown going over there. But what we do is offer people a chance to release their emotions, which is the first step to recovery. They laugh, they cry, they open up, they become more whole. These are places where people haven't seen a kid laugh for a month."

"Sure, you can build a hospital and get a plaque with your name on it," she says in response to the inevitable question, which is whether performing antics involving water balloons and papier-mâché masks is really the best way to aid war-ravaged populations. "And hospitals and infrastructure are part of what's needed," her husband chimes in. "But people need to be people. What we do lets kids dream. What we do lets them imagine a future."

Ms. Gelsone, Princeton class of '96, and Mr. Bloom, Wesleyan '98, were both children of first-generation Peace Corps volunteers. They learned their craft attending clown college and spent several years as a professional couple before becoming something more. "It's a cardinal rule—never date a clown partner," Ms. Gelsone explains. "You can find a date anywhere. But a clown partner? Not so easy." Not to mention the fact that in the country where they met, rules governing behavior between the sexes are so strict that even kissing in public is forbidden.

Then one day out of the blue, Mr. Bloom announced to Ms. Gelsone, "I want to spend the rest of my life with you," or words to that effect. To say she was stunned would be putting it mildly. "You don't want to flirt a little first?" she asked. But by the spring of 2007 they were living together, and that October they were married in a pageantlike ceremony in the Chinese city of Hangzhou for which Ms. Gelsone wore a dress made of white balloons. They honeymooned in the Wakhan Corridor of Afghanistan, one of the world's most remote corners, and the following May bought this co-op for about $260,000.

It's not surprising that a couple who spend their lives doing good works around the world would choose to live in a place shaped by a strong social agenda. Their apartment house, in a neighborhood where buildings were once outfitted with brass railings and presided over by doormen, had in recent decades fallen on hard times. But thanks to a municipal program under which rundown city-owned properties are renovated and the apartments made available to families whose annual earnings fall under a certain level, the building is enjoying a healthy second act. The goal is to help families of relatively limited means become home owners, and the impact in working-class minority neighborhoods like this one has been considerable.

For the couple, the program's ideological underpinnings were appealing, so much so that Mr. Bloom ended up as vice president of the co-op board. And for a pair who together earn $70,000 in a good year—clowning is hardly the world's most lucrative profession—the deal was appealing financially.

Unlike many parts of Harlem, these streets are yet to be gentrified, if gentrification ever arrives. Good Job Hair Braiding, El Chong Deli Grocery, and other of the mom-and-pop businesses that line the route to the couple's building suggest that the first Starbucks won't show up for a while. But Mr. Bloom and Ms. Gelsone are drawn to this unmanicured quality. People barbecue in the cement yards in the rear of their buildings and play salsa and hip-hop on the street. Neighbors in their apartment house are so chatty, it can take 15 minutes to collect the mail. "Where we travel, life happens on the street," Mr. Bloom explains. "This is more like the rest of our lives."

Within the apartment, everything contributes to helping them become better at what they do. To create a rehearsal area, they collapsed the three small front rooms into a single continuous expanse and redid the floors, each of which had been built at a slightly different level. They furnished the space with items from Ikea (cheap) and tatami mats (easily rolled up and stashed in a corner). During the day, when most of their neighbors are out, they can do handstands and pratfalls to their hearts' content. As a gentle homage to their time in China, they painted the kitchen red, gold, and blue, the colors of the Forbidden City in Beijing. "When Seth chose red kitchen cabinets," Ms. Gelsone says, "I thought to myself, 'Yes! I married the right guy!'"

And while the couple's professional center of gravity lies thousands of miles away, the apartment is filled with pictures and paraphernalia that evoke their life on the road. These include not only the clowning tools in the closet and the grinning papier-mâché masks that Mr. Bloom created using a plaster mold of his head but also the photographs that provide a vivid record of their travels.

The scenes of Afghanistan are especially moving. We see boys selling glasses of water for one afghani (two cents) apiece and others kicking around a soccer ball in front of the old palace in Kabul. We see men enjoying buzkashi, a traditional Central Asian sport that is played on horseback and involves tossing around a dead goat. In perhaps the most joyous image, a girl from a Kabul orphanage stands atop a pair of borrowed stilts, wearing an ankle-length dress that was specially made to cover her legs and gives her the appearance of a small red tent. She looks exultant, and according to Mr. Bloom, she was. "She was up there for four or five hours," he recalls. "She said she never wanted to come down."

# 16

## For a Writer, a Home with a Hideout

### Roxana Robinson and Her Husband on the Upper East Side

JULY 12, 2009

The novelist Roxana Robinson in her Classic 8 on the Upper East Side. (James Estrin/*The New York Times*)

THE novelist Roxana Robinson, who lives in a Classic 8 on the Upper East Side of Manhattan, can reel off many of the unusual ways that writers have found quiet and solitude in which to practice their craft. Ernest Hemingway holed up in a cheap apartment without electricity above a sawmill in Paris. The short-story writer Raymond Carver wrote in the front seat of his car, a pad balanced on his lap. When the essayist Annie Dillard, writing in the library in Hollins College, became overly fond of watching the comings and goings in the parking lot outside her window, she drew a sketch of the scene, closed the Venetian blinds, and taped the sketch onto the blinds.

Ms. Robinson, whose home is an 11-story red-brick apartment house on East 68th Street near Park Avenue, writes in an 8-by-10-square-foot space that faces a tan brick wall and was formerly a maid's room. In décor and design, the space is as spare as a monk's cell. The spartan furnishings include a brown wooden chair, a small white bureau, a cotton rug, and an old-fashioned metal radiator whose gray paint is peeling. A white coverlet lies atop a twin bed. The only possible distraction comes from the set of shelves filled with children's books for visiting youngsters. The first thing in the morning, after having had her coffee but before speaking to anyone, Ms. Robinson retreats to this room, sits cross-legged on the bed, places her laptop on her knees, and writes for several hours.

These austere quarters are hardly her only option. At the opposite end of the sprawling apartment, where she and her husband, Hamilton, a retired investment banker, have lived for 12 years, is a welcoming study that would seem the ideal lair for a novelist. This room is considerably larger than the onetime maid's quarters and combines the necessities of 21st-century life—computer, printer, fax machine—with immense personality, thanks to works of art and memorabilia that paint an indelible portrait of its occupant and her highly textured world.

Ms. Robinson, whose works include an acclaimed biography of the painter Georgia O'Keeffe and most recently the novel *Cost*, realizes that in choosing the unprepossessing small room over the more lavishly decorated larger one, she has rejected a space most writers would kill for. But over the years she has given a great deal of thought to why certain spaces encourage the writing life and others seem to inhibit it, and she has come to understand why she made the choice she did.

"I did everything *but* write in that room," Ms. Robinson says of the study. "I paid bills. I printed things out. I sent faxes. I was connected to the Internet. The assumption is that writers can write wherever they can sit down. But the main thing you need as a writer is a sense of certainty that you won't be interrupted."

Distance from the Internet is part of the issue, especially in these ultra-wired days, hence the popularity among writers of a device that temporarily blocks connection to the Web. Ms. Robinson herself says that her idea of freedom is turning off the Internet for a few hours. But having a physical space that offers minimal distraction is equally critical. Especially for a writer living in New York, distraction can be the unwelcome flip side of inspiration. The buzzy activity that invigorates and offers food for thought can make it impossible to concentrate.

The building where Ms. Robinson lives embodies both those elements. The Art Deco apartment house, which was constructed in 1931, sits in one of the most congested parts of the most congested borough. Yet once through the front door, past the owls, rabbits, and squirrels carved on the façade, residents enter a far more tranquil world. This is partly because the apartment house and its sister residence on East 67th Street frame a magnificent interior garden, a private oasis that the *AIA Guide to New York City* describes as "a dream."

The Robinsons moved to this apartment, which they bought for under $1 million, from a century-old farmhouse in Katonah, in Westchester County. And while Ms. Robinson doesn't find her study conducive to writing, the space is nonetheless immensely inviting, outfitted with an antique floral carpet, a brass daybed, and an armchair with a flouncy skirt. In the evening, light is provided by a 19th-century Staffordshire lamp in the shape of a horse that was a gift from a beloved aunt, Eleanor Barry, an editor of *Harper's Bazaar* in the 1930s. The garden that's invisible from the maid's room is visible from the window here, which is framed by bookcases.

As in many places where people have been accumulating art and keepsakes for decades, every item comes with a story. A drawing by Laurent de Brunhoff, an author of the Babar books, shows the Robinsons as charming elephants, the lady elephant wearing a choker exactly like one that Ms. Robinson owns. A photograph by Jill Krementz shows Ms. Robinson's daughter making pasta and was included in a book on children who cook. There's an Alfred Stieglitz photograph of O'Keeffe from the 1930s and a watercolor of Ms. Robinson's husband painting a watercolor.

Two framed postcards are especially meaningful. One is from John Updike, a writer Ms. Robinson cites as her most important influence and one to whose works her own have been compared. "What a pretty book," he says of her 1996 story collection *Asking for Love*. "Now you say I've been relevant to you and it's made my day." The other postcard, from the novelist Alice Munro, is equally complimentary: "Your book reached me here in Ireland and delighted me no end." The subject of these messages couldn't be more honored. "My two heroes," Ms. Robinson says, smiling at the images.

The sweeping living room is a reflection of Ms. Robinson's deep interest in early 20th-century American art; she began her career in the early 1970s at Sotheby's and in the mid-'70s wrote art history because she couldn't get her fiction published. Most arresting is a life-size oil of Ms. Robinson wearing a strapless black evening gown, much like the gown Madame X wore in John Singer Sargent's famous 1884 painting, and the same choker worn by the little elephant in the drawing in the study. The portrait is by the artist Ron Sherr, whose subsequent subjects included the first George Bush. On end tables sit vintage snuffboxes that the couple collect, along with a silver cigarette case that belonged to Ms. Robinson's father.

The opulence of these surroundings would be familiar to many of Ms. Robinson's characters. Her subject matter is typically the world of the WASP, a world of financial ease and physical comfort. Her characters would feel at home amid all these lovely things. Yet the search for the austere cork-lined room that Proust extolled has been a continuing theme in Ms. Robinson's life, so much so that once she seriously considered carving a writer's room out of the apartment's basement storage area. The windowless cell, the same size as the maid's room, was lined with cement block and furnished with a three-legged table and other ailing castoffs, but it had a certain appeal. "It was clean and well maintained," Ms. Robinson says, "not full of spiders. I wouldn't have heard the phone." Only the lack of ventilation made her hesitate.

During her years in Katonah, the search for a room of her own, the space that Virginia Woolf extolled more than three-quarters of a century ago, was especially consuming. "For a writer not to have a real room in which to write is like a lawyer working in his pajamas and trying to put the sound of a three-piece suit in his voice," Ms. Robinson says. "When I was starting out, only in my imagination was I a writer. I worked in a tiny bedroom at my husband's childhood desk. It was as if I didn't dare take over the whole room."

She wrote the O'Keeffe biography on a card table, in a guest room furnished with a big double bed. When her husband, as a birthday present, redid the top of the garage to create a study for his wife, she was thrilled.

The search for a suitable place to work is an issue for every writer. But for women, as Woolf understood better than anyone, the issue is especially fraught. "When you're in the house," Ms. Robinson points out, "you're shaped by the house. You know that you're in charge, that you're literally the housekeeper. So to take over part of the house for your own use feels kind of arrogant. Your real position is as wife, as mother, as cook. When you're working at home, you're always balancing your writing with household tasks like washing the dishes. And so it feels strange to create a person in the house that doesn't relate to the house. You're always wondering, who am I really?"

Even on vacation in Maine, Ms. Robinson's search for a cocoon in which she can be as solitary as possible continues. "I have a beautiful study there, with a view of the water," she says, "but when I'm really working, toward the end of a book, I abandon it and go into a dark sort of attic space, under the eaves, with no view and no phone, no machines, nothing but floor space and silence."

# 17

# Where Wit Pays the Rent

## Carolita Johnson and Michael Crawford in Inwood

NOVEMBER 22, 2009

Carolita Johnson and Michael Crawford, New Yorker cartoonists, in their prewar apartment in Washington Heights. (Tina Fineberg for *The New York Times*)

CAROLITA JOHNSON, a 44-year-old illustrator, model, and *New Yorker* cartoonist, has lived in some appalling places. During a 15-year sojourn in Paris, she occupied garrets with no toilet, no heat, no hot water, and no shower (she used the municipal baths). In New York, she lived in a $500-a-month closet in Dumbo, followed by an apartment in Harlem beset by security problems, heating problems, and what Ms. Johnson diplomatically calls critters. The buildings on her street were such a mess, the director John Cassavetes had used one of them to film *Gloria*, his gritty tale of mobsters and other lowlifes.

So Ms. Johnson was understandably delighted last spring when she and Michael Crawford, a painter and fellow *New Yorker* cartoonist, moved into a sunny three-bedroom in Inwood, in a 1920 building that retains much of its prewar panache. The apartment, which they rent for $2,300 a month, sits at the northern tip of Riverside Drive, and its amenities include two marble bathrooms, a view of the Cloisters and Fort Tryon Park, and enough room for his-and-hers studios.

Other than their gifts as cartoonists and their matching black-rimmed glasses, the two occupants couldn't be less alike, at least in terms of their background. Ms. Johnson, who has long dark hair and a model's willowy figure, grew up in Queens, the child of an Ecuadorean mother and a father from New Jersey. The first neighborhood in which her family lived was comfortably multiethnic Flushing; the next one, Little Neck, which sits on the Long Island border, was less welcoming. Ms. Johnson couldn't escape fast enough.

After studying at Parsons School of Design, she made her way to Europe, where she worked as a model in London and Paris, and, while in Paris, pursued various lofty-sounding academic studies. She received a master's degree in comparative literature with a minor in linguistics and wrote a thesis titled "Rape (Specifically the Rape of Lucrece) as a Rhetorical Figure in Political Discourse from Antiquity to Shakespeare"—not the sort of thing you skim to kill time at the hair salon.

In 2002, after abandoning doctoral studies in medieval anthropology, Ms. Johnson returned to New York to pursue a career as an illustrator. Shortly thereafter, she was introduced to the silver-haired Mr. Crawford by a mutual friend from *The New Yorker*. Mr. Crawford, 20 years her senior, had grown up on the shores of Lake Ontario, in Oswego, New York. His Canadian-born mother was a painter and a German teacher, and his father was an assemblyman and later a judge. Now divorced, he has two grown children.

Mr. Crawford and Ms. Johnson became friends by way of his admiration for her work. "She had a great drawing style," he says, and he was convinced that *The New Yorker* would welcome her offbeat wit. He encouraged her to submit cartoons for the magazine, and his instincts about her talent proved sound. It had taken him six years to sell his first drawing to *The New Yorker*; she told hers in five weeks. Ms. Johnson also has a lucrative day job working as a fitting model, which has the ancillary benefit of getting her out of the apartment at odd hours. This is good, she says, "because having different schedules is conducive to domestic tranquility."

The couple are not married; in fact, they were initially so discreet about their relationship that many of their *New Yorker* colleagues had no idea that they were an item. But they sometimes refer to each other as husband and wife, and as Ms. Johnson describes the arrangement, "We just like to say that by the power invested in Michael and Carolita, we pronounced ourselves Michael and Carolita."

And their home isn't perfect. Though the building has a spacious lobby with tile floors and radiates a genial faded charm, the apartment shows its age. The kitchen cabinets are gently askew, and the slightly angled living room ceilings make it a challenge to hang pictures properly, no small issue for a pair of artists. Given the drawbacks, it's hard to put your finger on what qualities give this place such appeal. Maybe it's the pleasant surprise of finding such a bright and cheerful outpost so far from the heart of the city. Stolid Inwood, historically the home of Jewish émigrés and working-class Irish families, has hardly been a destination neighborhood for artists or much of anyone. But in recent years, as Manhattan and even Brooklyn have been gripped by a housing crunch, once-lackluster neighborhoods like Inwood that offer prewar sturdiness at price levels manageable even for members of the creative class are increasingly alluring.

With rooms that flow gracefully into one another and are bright with sunshine much of the day, this space is ideal for a pair of artists. They in turn have transformed their quarters into what one cartoonist friend described as "a wonderful apartment thick with paint and ink and exuberance." The wit and warmth that characterizes their work seems to overflow from their inkpots and spill into every corner.

The view is a special draw. In spring and summer everything is green with white blossoms, in autumn the landscape is red and gold, and in winter the couple can see the boulders of the park and, in the distance, the gray tower of the Cloisters. "There's always a view," Ms. Johnson says. "It's like a fourth room."

For a passionate cook, the kitchen is the heart of a house; for a gardener, it's the backyard. For artists, studios are what matter, and it would be hard to picture rooms more conducive to creativity than the work spaces in this apartment. They're so welcoming, with so many things to catch the eye, you're not surprised that good work emanates from these drawings boards.

In Mr. Crawford's studio, the larger of the two and the one with the better view, paintings perch on an easel and cover much of the wall space. Fat tubes of oil paints carpet the floor, glass jars hold a small army of brushes and colored pencils, and the drawers of a storage chest bear whimsical labels like "desktop detritus/paints." Among the array of portraits, landscapes, and nudes is a drawing titled *My Central Park*, a rendition of the city's most famous green space that includes such locations as "Pale Shirtless Depressives Hill," "Skateboard Hell," "Bad Jazz Pergola," "The Lake of Colliding Boats," and "The Great Public Displays of Affection Lawn."

Ms. Johnson's studio, reached by passing through French doors, is home to an equally eclectic assortment of images, among them a drawing titled *Birds of Central Park*, done for the Web site Gothamist and featuring the "wingless pigeon." (That would be a rat.) Ms. Johnson's studio also accommodates the couple's bikes and her banjo (she recently began taking lessons from the bluegrass player Tony Trischka) and feels cozy, thanks to deep-purple African violets and a white sheepskin rug beloved by the couple's dog, Hammett. But do not think that these two are homebodies who never leave their drawing boards. Those bikes get lots of use, and thanks to Hammett, the couple visit the park every day. In addition, both are members of the *New Yorker* softball team. She plays right field, he plays first base, and they store their bats in a golf bag parked in a corner of the living room.

Yet returning home never disappoints. And especially for Ms. Johnson, with so many terrible apartments in her past, any crookedness of cabinet or lopsidedness of ceiling is no deal-breaker. "I lived in so many awful places," she says. "I used to be terrified of opening the oven door because I'd find mice there."

# 18

# The Art of Sparkle

## Elizabeth Lewis in Murray Hill

DECEMBER 9, 2009

Elizabeth Lewis, a jewelry designer, in a one-bedroom in Murray Hill that converts into a showroom. (Chester Higgins Jr./*The New York Times*)

WITH carved stonework, trailing ivy, and imitation gaslight lanterns, the brownstones of East 35th Street between Park and Lexington Avenues seem frozen in another era. Suspend disbelief for a moment, and you wouldn't be the least surprised if a couple out of Edith Wharton rounded the corner, she in a flowing dress, he in a cutaway coat, and the two of them discussing 13-course dinners featuring terrapin ducks. It's understandable that the novelist chose this neighborhood for a pivotal setting in *The Age of Innocence*: the town house that Newland Archer's father-in-law purchased for Archer and his bride, May Welland, was located just blocks away, on East 39th Street.

Elizabeth Lewis, a 38-year-old jewelry designer who works with rock crystal, rose quartz, green onyx, and other semiprecious stones, is hardly a character out of Wharton, nor, one suspects, would she care to be. But to enter one of these turn-of-the-last-century buildings and climb the two winding flights that lead to her apartment is to step into a similarly alluring world.

Because Ms. Lewis can't afford separate quarters in which to make and sell her creations, her apartment does triple duty as home, work space, and showroom. During the day, the pendants, chains, and earrings that she laboriously fashions by hand glitter in the sun that pours through the large window in the living room. At night, under the inviting glow of the brass chandelier and matching sconces, these same items look rich and festive. It's a cliché to say that walking into this little apartment is like stepping into a jewel box, but the image is irresistible. And Ms. Lewis herself, dressed one weekday morning in a strapless black dress set off by long gold earrings and a crystal pendant on a thin gold chain, both of her own design, makes you think for a second of the tiny twirling ballerinas that sometimes inhabit such settings.

No one who knew Ms. Lewis as a lively, dark-haired girl growing up in suburban New Jersey would be surprised to learn that she ended up as a designer. She was a creative child: She wrote poetry; she studied ballet. But when she came to New York in 1994, six days after graduating from college, her first job had more to do with profit-and-loss statements than with making pretty things. "I worked as a junior account executive for Donna Karan, and I spent most of my time sitting in front of an Excel spreadsheet, crunching," she says. "That was definitely not where I saw myself."

There followed a stint as a sales assistant at Calvin Klein's Madison Avenue boutique, after which she took time off to care for her ailing mother. Her moment of truth, so to speak, came shortly after her mother died in 1999. "A friend of my father reminded me that I was approaching 30," Ms. Lewis says. "He told me that although I wanted to do something creative, and that was nice as a hobby, I should do it on the side and make some money." Still raw from her mother's death, this was the last piece of advice she cared to hear. "But he swayed me with his tough love," she says of the family friend. A month later, she went to work for him doing Web-site development, and she stayed for four years.

Yet the urge to live a more creative life had not disappeared. It had simply gone underground, awaiting the proper moment to reemerge. Despite the lack of any formal training, Ms. Lewis began "playing around with beads," as she puts it, and hanging out in the bead district located in the West 30s and 40s. (Leave it to New York, with its scores of microcommercial neighborhoods, to have a bead district.) One day, she walked into a shop, bought some beads and wire, and asked a small, shy woman in the back what to do with them. "They didn't have an abundance of tools, but she took a liking to me and gave me hers," Ms. Lewis recalls. "She said, 'They're old and need replacing anyway.'"

In the beginning, she simply made things for herself and people she knew, "giving them away, or charging $25, whatever." Then, at a friend's urging, she held a cocktail party at which a few guests modeled her creations. Ms. Lewis had been skeptical of the idea; overcome with panic at 3 a.m. the previous night, she'd been ready to cancel the whole thing, convinced that no one other than family and close friends would come and anxious about how her work would be received. But despite misgivings, she went ahead with the event, and she would be glad that she did. More than a hundred people showed up and in a three-hour period bought more than $10,000 worth of merchandise. Within a month, Ms. Lewis was making jewelry full-time, and a business was born.

Two years ago, perhaps empowered by her growing professional success, she made another change in her life. Ms. Lewis had been living on the Upper East Side, in an apartment depressingly near the hospital where her mother had died. In an effort to avoid daily reminders of those difficult months, she moved to this one-bedroom in Murray Hill.

The downsides were its size—just 540 square feet—and the rent, which at $3,000 a month was hardly cheap for someone trying to grow a business. But the upsides were considerable and included its proximity to the bead district along with architectural and decorative details that like the street itself speak to the graciousness of an earlier New York. The apartment is outfitted with 12-foot ceilings, a brick-lined fireplace, decorative moldings applied with a lavish hand, original wood floors, and window seats overlooking the street. The chandelier and sconces came with the apartment, as did the glass-paned pocket doors leading to the bedroom. May Welland would have felt at home.

Partly so that visitors can admire prospective purchases, mirrors lurk everywhere, among them some with gilded frames that came from the house in which Ms. Lewis grew up. And because the apartment functions as a public space as much as a private one, she has tried to keep signs of domestic activity to a minimum. The beige marble bathroom, accented with votive candles, is so pristine, it's hard to imagine that anyone so much as powdered a nose there. The black Parsons table that doubles as a desk is neater than floor models in stores. On the platform bed, which is covered with a pale-sea-foam-green comforter, pillows are nowhere in evidence because, as Ms. Lewis explains, "I wanted a bed that didn't scream bed." It's fortunate that the apartment's occupant rarely cooks, because the kitchen cabinets are stocked not with canisters of rice and pasta but with leatherette neck forms, satin pouches, silken cord, lengths of gold chain, and 10 pairs of pliers, all of different sizes. The oven, an appliance that will never see a roast chicken or a batch of cookies, is stuffed with serving trays and Champagne glasses.

When it comes time for Ms. Lewis to display her work to guests, the stage is reset. She invites a hundred or more people, breaks out the festive glassware, buys roses from the corner deli, and serves Veuve Clicquot, crudités, cupcakes, "and maybe a little candy for color." Counters and tabletops glitter with examples of her creations—letter-charm necklaces, double-drop rock-crystal-quartz pendants that are a favorite bridesmaid's gift, dangling black onyx earrings, and long necklaces hung with tiny golden stars. Judging by the comments on her Web site, her creations are finding an audience. "My beautiful blue topaz earrings arrived this afternoon—and I am simply thrilled," one customer wrote. "They are even lovelier than I had remembered. I expect them to be part of my life forever."

Living and working in the same small space can have drawbacks, especially when the work is labor-intensive and often solitary. "Sometimes, the job takes over," Ms. Lewis admits. "You're never off duty.

And it can be very quiet and lonely here." Hence the appeal of her gym, where she has recently taken up yoga. Hence also the appeal of a new boyfriend, a furniture designer and painter who understands the demands of the creative life. Previous boyfriends were mostly lawyers or men who worked in finance. "Not that there's anything wrong with that," Ms. Lewis adds hastily. "But I'm better off with this guy."

# 19

# Her Second Home, the One without Wheels

## Kim Ima in the West Village

**FEBRUARY 21, 2010**

Kim Ima, creator of the Treats Truck, in her West Village one-bedroom.
(Michael Appleton for *The New York Times*)

BACK in the 1970s, one of the staples of New York starter apartments was a poster advertising rye bread, an image that featured a member of a decidedly non-Jewish ethnic group—Asian, American Indian, African-American—along with the tagline "You don't have to be Jewish to love Levy's." But if there's any place where the poster is an appropriate item of décor, it's the West Village apartment of Kim Ima, a half-Japanese (on her father's side), half-Jewish (on her mother's side) transplant from California who has given New York the Treats Truck, one of the most beloved purveyors of street food. If you've ever seen a smiling woman in a gray vehicle with red, white, and blue accents dispensing raspberry-topped brownies and Rice Krispies squares on a New York street corner, you're familiar with this institution.

Ms. Ima's version of the poster, featuring an Asian boy gazing solemnly at an enormous rye-bread sandwich, occupies a prominent spot in her one-bedroom apartment on Bank Street. And perched on the desk opposite sits a photograph of her late maternal grandparents, Rose and Richard Miller, a reminder that Ms. Ima's familial roots in the city run deep. Mr. Miller grew up here, and around the turn of the last century, his father, Ruben, operated a pushcart on the Lower East Side.

"We think he sold pots and pans," Ms. Ima says—not quite sugary concoctions like oatmeal jammies, chocolate chippers, or sugar dots, three of the Treats Truck's more delectably named items, but evidence that hawking merchandise from a vehicle on the streets of New York runs in the family.

Ms. Ima, who is 42 but looks a decade younger, was raised in San Diego. Yet New York always held a fascination for her. When she was little, her grandfather used to tell her stories about Charlotte Russes he bought on the Lower East Side, and as a child, she tried to replicate this iconic New York pastry, carefully tucking ladyfingers and custard into tiny paper cups.

In 1991, after graduating from U.C.L.A., Ms. Ima moved to New York, where she earned a master of fine arts degree from Columbia and plunged into a career as an actor and dancer. A role that held special meaning involved a project by a Seattle troupe about the internment camps to which Japanese-Americans, including her father and other relatives, had been confined during the Second World War. But it was in New York that she found her true professional home. In 1996, she made her way to La MaMa, the venerable downtown theater company where she ultimately spent a decade working as a performer and a director. And thanks in part to La MaMa she embarked upon what would become the robust second chapter of her career.

Baking had always been a part of Ms. Ima's life; those Charlotte Russes were just the beginning. "I have very warm memories of baked goods as a way of reaching out to people," she says, and even more than most little girls, she treasured the experience of making chocolate-chip cookies with her mother on rainy days. Yet only when she started whipping up brownies for La MaMa's hungry players, a group notable for minimal incomes combined with appetites sharpened by intense physical labor, did she realize that baking for a crowd might be more than a hobby.

"I was obsessed," she says of this period in her life. "I'd have baking parties, and dinner parties where we had seven courses, all of them desserts." Some concoctions were great. Others, notably those involving Jell-O, somewhat less so. But the effort made her feel, she says, "like a grown-up Girl Scout, working for the world's biggest merit badge." And something that Ellen Stewart, La MaMa's legendary founder and a mentor to Ms. Ima, used to say, perhaps metaphorically, resonated deeply: "She'd say to me, 'You need your own pushcart.' Now I tell people, 'I've found my cart.'" The Treats Truck opened in 2007 and the following year was honored with a Vendy, an award as cherished as a Tony by the city's street-food vendors.

Around the time Ms. Ima joined La MaMa, she also made a major change in her domestic life, ending a nomadic existence that had involved bouncing around among half a dozen rentals and sublets. In 1996, with the help of her supportive parents, she bought this third-floor apartment, in a postwar building near Greenwich Street, for $150,000.

Given that the Treats Truck was born in the space, you'd expect the kitchen to be both spacious and jaw-droppingly high-tech. Although for a fleeting moment before arriving in this apartment Ms. Ima had visions of a kitchen large enough for a whole gang of friends to hang out, this one is neither large nor glitzy. When she started testing recipes, she did so in a space the size of a pocket handkerchief, using a black and white enamel Royal Rose gas stove that seems to have wandered over from some rich little girl's dollhouse. The Royal Rose now sits primly in a corner, replaced by a sleek new Viking. "But the Royal Rose isn't going anywhere," she says. She uses the top as a drying rack and stores birthday cakes and potholders in the minuscule oven.

The kitchen offers a visual primer on cooking and serving traditions of the past century. Vintage aprons trimmed with rickrack and stitched from flowered pastels that went out of fashion decades ago hang on pegs like homespun works of art. Shelves are heaped with such winsome odds and ends as old-fashioned eggbeaters with Bakelite handles, '50s-era milk bottles, red and gold Melmac bowls, and salt and pepper shakers shaped like baby toasters. Posters for products like Postum and Carnation evaporated milk, rarely seen in contemporary kitchens, adorn the walls.

Shelves above Ms. Ima's desk accommodate her collection of cookbooks, many of which are for young people, along with children's storybooks with charming titles like *What's in the Bakery Truck?* and *The Story of Cherry the Pig*, whose protagonist sails off with honors in a baking contest thanks to her delectable apple cake. The books share space with 11 cheerful-looking jars of ancient Marshmallow Fluff, not to be consumed, God knows—"There's no way I'd eat old Marshmallow Fluff," Ms. Ima announces firmly—but because she loves the labels.

Although the apartment's windows mostly face brick walls, Ms. Ima has compensated for the lack of natural light by infusing dollops of charm and color, and her personality is writ large on every wall and tabletop. A swath of patterned fabric paying homage to the Barbie doll drapes the sofa. A stuffed animal perches atop an upright Electrolux vacuum rescued from the street. A light-up plastic goose, a gift from a friend, presides in a corner. Glitter-splashed wallpaper lines an entire wall. Culinary accents take the form of plastic doughnuts ("because you've got to love plastic food") and a lazy Susan shaped like a giant lemon slice that Ms. Ima inherited from her grandmother Rose. "If there's a fire," she says, "that's what I'll grab first."

When Ms. Ima moved to this apartment, she was part of a couple, but after five years of living together, she and her longtime boyfriend parted. She is without regrets and in fact is proud that once single, she proceeded to make the place her own. She is also proud that she is living not as a grad student or as part of a twosome "but as a single adult, as a grown-up." She wonders if the breakup was the spark that propelled her forward.

Whatever the explanation, the result is very cozy, although as the sole owner of a demanding and time-consuming business, the apartment's occupant spends little time here. Being the main driver and seller, her workdays begin at 6 or 7 a.m., when she heads off to the Treats Truck kitchen in Red Hook, Brooklyn, to supervise a crew of bakers already up to their elbows in flour. She also picks up her truck, a vehicle that she stations at various locations in Manhattan.

Because Ms. Ima's workday ends 10 to 15 hours later, and this is her schedule most days of the week, she savors coming home to a welcoming setting. "I like having a place to nest," she says. "And it's probably lucky that I got it fixed up before the Treats Truck started, so I already had a lovely home to come back to at the end of the day." Otherwise, she realizes, she would never have had the time.

# 20

# Magic Moments

## Rory Feldman and His Mother in Homecrest, Brooklyn

JUNE 27, 2010

Rory Feldman, a magician and collector of memorabilia related to the magician Howard Thurston, in Hillcrest, Brooklyn. (Nicole Bengiveno/*The New York Times*)

"**P**ICK a card, any card," Rory Feldman instructs a visitor as he stands in the living room of his Brooklyn apartment and extends a well-thumbed deck. When the visitor chooses the three of clubs, Mr. Feldman tears off one corner, marks the back of the card with an X and the visitor's initials, folds the card into a tiny square, and clenches it in his fist. Seconds later, the marked card reappears on a nearby shelf, tucked inside a worn brown leather wallet with the name Howard Thurston embossed in gold.

The spirit of Thurston, a turn-of-the-last-century illusionist who wasn't ashamed to call himself "the world's greatest magician," looms over this room. From the colorful vintage posters that line the walls, so close to one another that they're practically touching, a somber-faced man with sensitive dark eyes stares down at Mr. Feldman as if silently urging him on. Thurston's image is refracted endlessly in hundreds of photographs and programs that fill floor-to-ceiling display cabinets, as if this modest living room deep in the heart of Brooklyn were a carnival funhouse of mirrors. In one image, in which the magician's matinee-idol looks are set off by a glossy black jacket with a carnation in the lapel, Thurston gazes almost adoringly at a skull he holds in his hands. "Do the spirits come back?" the title wonders.

When people think of the golden age of magic—the late 19th and early 20th centuries—the name Harry Houdini invariably comes to mind, along with a mental picture of a muscular man untangling himself from a prison of chains. But in Mr. Feldman's opinion, magic's true virtuoso was a largely forgotten Midwesterner whose act was described as "the wonder show of the universe" and whose proficiency with cards was second to none.

"Houdini, who was primarily an escape artist, was impressive but no rival," says Mr. Feldman, a 29-year-old magician and passionate collector of all things Thurston. "Thurston, though, was the master of his craft. He was a superstar—everyone who saw him said so. They said he was likable, funny, that he loved his audience. He performed for poor children, for orphans, for crippled children." Mr. Feldman finds it tragic that few people remember his name.

Thurston was born in 1869 in Columbus, Ohio, lived for a time in Whitestone, Queens, and died in Miami in 1936 at the age of 66. But if any place honors his memory, it's this two-bedroom apartment on East

17th Street, in a neighborhood officially known as Homecrest but described by many residents as Midwood. Here Mr. Feldman has established a shrine to his idol. The living room is dominated by his collection of 18,000 items—props, costumes, programs, instructional manuals—arranged in those custom-built display cabinets, one of which extends the length of a long wall. More than 100 scrapbooks are stuffed with photographs, lithographs, archival material, and ephemera. An honest-to-God museum couldn't be more comprehensive or have been created with more passion.

Mr. Feldman grew up in this apartment, which is located in a small postwar building, and shares the space with his mother, Suzanne, who moved in as a bride in 1974. Less than a decade later, at 31, Ms. Feldman's husband died, leaving her with two young sons, Rory, then 2, and his 4-year-old brother, Morgan. She stayed in the apartment, for which she now pays $1,500 in rent, and so did her younger child.

Not every mother would relish sharing her home with a long-dead illusionist. But Ms. Feldman insists that she has grown fond of the individual who's virtually a third member of the household. "Years ago, of course, the living room was decorated differently," says Ms. Feldman, who teaches prekindergarten in the same classroom where her younger son was a pupil nearly a quarter of a century ago. "But Rory's collection gives the room such appeal—all the colors and Thurston wearing all the different expressions. He's like a member of my family. And of course, Rory is a walking encyclopedia. He's the master."

Mr. Feldman was 3 when he received a Fisher-Price magic set as a gift and discovered what would be his life's passion. Lots of boys enjoy an early flirtation with magic, but for the young Rory, the power to amaze his elders with his tricks proved seductive, or, as he puts it, "It makes you feel you have a power." By the age of 8, he was earning up to $100 a gig for performing at birthday parties; his mother used to drive him and his props to his events. By the age of 12, he was wowing his fellow sixth graders with "Eggs Extraordinary," a signature Thurston trick in which the magician pulled one egg after another out of a silk top hat, using Thurston's own top hat for his performance. He began collecting apparatus, and as he started buying and selling seriously, Thurston became his passion.

Along with his mother, and of course Thurston, a fixture in the apartment is Mr. Feldman's girlfriend, a book editor named Cara Bedick. The couple met as teenagers when they were camp counselors, and she spends much of her free time here. "We've been together for 11 years," Mr. Feldman says. "She's very understanding of all the baggage I bring to the relationship."

New York is famously a city of obsessives and obsessions, home to people who lead unlikely lives behind the city's closed doors: who can forget the transit buff from Sheepshead Bay whose bedroom was dominated by the motorman's cab from an old subway car? It's tempting to dismiss Mr. Feldman as a member of their ranks, and he himself acknowledges that not everyone lives as he lives. "I realize my collection takes over the apartment," he says. "But my mom's so supportive. She sees such a passion. And if she doesn't like a particular item, we just hide it."

Mr. Feldman's enthusiasm is contagious. After a few hours in his presence, it's easy to sense the appeal of Thurston's slightly spooky world, to feel that he has been wrongly assigned to the dustbin of history, and to applaud Mr. Feldman's efforts to rescue him.

These efforts are considerable. Mr. Feldman's collection includes props for myriad tricks, many with delectable names like "The Vanishing Whippet." A display features the bird cage, light bulb, and hammer used for a complicated trick called "The Canary and Light Bulb" in which a canary miraculously survives a near-death experience.

Mr. Feldman also owns a painted box from which Thurston made a rabbit magically appear and a pan that Thurston used to whip up an unusual cake: he would toss in flour and sugar, then close the lid, and when he removed the lid, a flock of doves and pigeons flew out. Other items help us picture what a dashing figure Thurston must have cut onstage, among them his tailcoat with fancy buttons, his white tuxedo shirt, his octagonal gold and silver cufflinks, and his beaver-skin top hat, still slightly shiny after more than a century. Nearby are the outfit of black and white feathers worn by Thurston's daughter, Jane, who helped him in his acts, and a faded red velvet chair in which the magician's assistant used to "vanish in plain sight," as Mr. Feldman describes this particular illusion.

Despite the preponderance of Thurstoniana, Mr. Feldman's mother has retained a few pieces recalling a life that doesn't involve top hats and disappearing playing cards. A mahogany grandfather clock that was a wedding present stands near the front door. A hand-painted blue and turquoise vase that dates back to 1858 and belonged to her parents sits on a living room table. But Thurston is the main event and, for Mr. Feldman, a full-time job. He earns his living buying, selling, and performing, and his great hope is that his collection will one day be part of an official

Museum of Magic, an institution he has already taken legal steps to establish.

If the museum finds a home and the collection departs for another location, will Ms. Feldman feel elated or bereft? "Hopefully, some of the stuff will stay," she says. "Rory's a good boy, my best friend. He knows how I feel about all this stuff. He knows they can't take my Thurston away."

# 21

# Caretakers of a Culture

## LuLu LoLo and Dan Evans in East Harlem

AUGUST 22, 2010

LuLu LoLo, a performance artist, and her husband, Dan Evans, a playwright and artist, in their 19th-century town house in East Harlem. (Ozier Muhammad/*The New York Times*)

FOR decades, the signs along East 116th Street have touted cheap airfare to San Juan and Mexico City. Restaurants and bodegas hawk cuchifritos and tacos. Salsa is the music of the streets. Except for culinary landmarks like Rao's and Patsy's, along with venerable institutions like Our Lady of Mount Carmel Church, the great stone church on East 115th Street, little survives from the days East Harlem reigned as the city's largest and most vibrant Italian-American neighborhood.

The Italian immigrants who began flooding the area in the late 19th century are largely gone, along with most of their descendants. A newspaper article published a few years ago about the neighborhood's fading Italian presence noted that fewer than a thousand Italian-Americans remained in East Harlem, that Mount Carmel stopped holding Italian-language masses several years earlier and the church's lone surviving Italian-American priest was 90 and bedridden. "They used to come back for weddings," a Spanish-speaking priest at Mount Carmel said of the older generation of congregants. "Now they just come for funerals." Yet that all-but-vanished world survives in the brick and brownstone town house on East 116th Street where LuLu LoLo and Dan Evans have lived for more than 35 years.

Encrusted as it is with relics of the past, their house is not everyone's cup of tea. As you move from room to room, you almost expect to hear period music from hidden loudspeakers or snatches of conversation from iconic immigrant events, perhaps the clamor of families arriving at Ellis Island. It's no surprise to learn that LuLu LoLo is obsessed with the obituaries of strangers, especially those who died in obscurity. Every so often a ceiling collapses, wearied by age, and there's nothing chic about the coffin in the parlor. Yet this homage to a largely forgotten past is unexpectedly affecting.

A noted judge named Joseph Boccia owned the house until his death in the 1960s. Boccia represented a link to the days when the fiery congressman Vito Marcantonio ruled these streets—he was a pallbearer at Marcantonio's funeral in 1954—and his initials are traced in black wrought iron on the front door. Photographs of LuLu LoLo's parents, Pete and Rose Pascale, are tucked into the metalwork. In the rooms beyond, a virtual-reality version of the old neighborhood endures as if enclosed in a bell jar.

This is largely thanks to LuLu LoLo, a performance artist who, not surprisingly, started out as the far more prosaic Lois Pascale and arrived at her stage name by way of a grandmother to whom she was always LuLu. Her roots in this part of the city run deep. Her grandparents emigrated from small towns in southern Italy, and her parents, pillars of the community, lived their entire lives in East Harlem, the neighborhood where LuLu LoLo grew up in the 1950s.

Her father died in 1997, her mother last year. Her father especially was a mythic figure in the neighborhood, so revered that her street bears his name. His obituary in *The New York Times* described him as a man "who loved East Harlem so much he made it the focus of his life, his work, his dreams and his memories."

LuLu LoLo and Mr. Evans were married in 1965, and in 1973, by then parents of three young sons, they bought the four-story building on East 116th Street from the judge's aged widow for $15,000. Only because the widow trusted Pete Pascale, with his impeccable neighborhood credentials, did she agree to be pried away from her family home. The house stood opposite the tenement where LuLu LoLo's mother lived as a child.

In those years, buying property in East Harlem struck most people as an act of insanity, even for a son or daughter of these streets. "The neighborhood in those years was terrible," LuLu LoLo recalls on a summer afternoon, sitting in the rear garden that was a wasteland when the couple arrived. "The crime, the heroin. We heard gunshots all the time." Her husband nods. "Everyone told us we were crazy," he says almost proudly. "No one was buying houses here in those years."

Although the house has endured considerable wear and tear since its construction in 1899, many original details survive, among them the cherry-wood banister and a wrought-iron chandelier. The ruddy brick walls are tastefully exposed. And over the decades, the house has evolved into a showcase for the couple's work. Mr. Evans is a playwright and a painter, and his black-and-white acrylics depicting scenes from classic movies like *China Seas* with Clark Gable and Jean Harlow line the walls. His wife's résumé describes her as a playwright, actress, visual artist, and especially performance artist, and in her professional photographs she looks quite theatrical, with deep-set eyes, crimson lips, and an exploding mop of black hair. A doll by the artist Timothy D. Bellavia outfitted with purple yarn hair and huge eyelashes nails the look perfectly. "That's her," Mr. Evans says, beaming at his wife.

Also on display is LuLu LoLo's remarkable collection of headgear, all of her own making. For her performances, she has concocted an assortment of fantastical collagelike headdresses, using found objects of every description—an aluminum faucet, a Cleveland Indians balloon, a stuffed bear for a Valentine's Day chapeau. One headdress, which she calls "Murder Mystery" and which features a passport, a string of pearls, a white glove, a cigarette, a pair of handcuffs, and a cute little gun, is an item Agatha Christie might have admired had she gone in for this sort of thing.

Most remarkable, however, is how intensely these rooms recall the days when East Harlem was the city's second Little Italy, starting with a tableau of black-and-white photographs of LuLu LoLo's ancestors in the narrow front hall. In a picture of a family dinner, a serious-looking child at the far end of the table gazes at the assortment of relatives and heaping platters of food; even at a tender age, the future LuLu LoLo was observing the world with a gimlet eye. Here too is her parents' wedding picture, dating from 1938. Their spirits hover over these rooms.

As a playwright and actress, LuLu LoLo has written and performed six one-woman plays, many of which feature individuals whose lives recall an increasingly forgotten immigrant world. Among the characters she has portrayed are two young Italian-American girls from East 119th Street who died in the Triangle shirtwaist factory fire, an event that looms large in her personal iconography. The cardboard Singer sewing machine she used for that project sits on a shelf and will make a repeat appearance when the centennial of the fire is marked next spring.

LuLu LoLo has also portrayed the Italian-born Mother Frances Xavier Cabrini, a venerated local figure who tended to the sick and was the first American citizen to be made a saint. To bring Mother Cabrini to life, she created a hospital bed, modeled after a 15th-century cradle at the Metropolitan Museum, and topped it with lace coverlets crocheted by her grandmother and studded with beads and crystals.

The second floor is home to what LuLu LoLo describes as her Paris room, a tribute to the city she adores almost as much as New York. Tabletop models of the Eiffel Tower are strung with Christmas lights, pastel boxes that once held Ladurée's macaroons line the shelves, and a miniature tricolor rustles in the breeze from the front window.

If the Paris room is LuLu LoLo's lair, the backyard is her husband's province, and he loves to tell how it came to be. That first summer in the house, his best friend, Tom Yeomans from Massachusetts, visited and wanted to buy Mr. Evans an almond tree in honor of their closeness. The choice of tree was inspired by the Nikos Kazantzakis novel *Report to Greco*, which had been important in both their lives, notably the scene in which St. Francis speaks to an almond tree and it bursts into bloom. So they went to a nursery to buy an almond tree. Were they crazy? the nurseryman demanded. Almond trees didn't grow in New York. Long story short, the two friends ended up with a crabapple that the nurseryman described as a dwarf and that's now 40 feet tall.

Nor is the crabapple alone. Four years ago, inspired by the fact that St. Francis used to live in a little hut, Mr. Yeomans's son Ben designed and built a small Gothic-style chapel that has been christened the Crabapple Chapel. Inside, containers hold the ashes of departed pets.

Though the purple irises that Judge Boccia loved are long gone, the garden is a respite regardless of season. Mr. Evans feeds peanuts to the squirrels. His wife watches fireflies against the night sky. Along with the burbling fountains they found in thrift shops, the garden also accommodates a veritable aviary. "We see woodpeckers, cardinals, hawks, mourning doves," LuLu LoLo says. "Once I saw a pheasant asleep on the roof of the chapel." Her husband goes her one better. "Once," he adds, "a neighbor saw a raccoon in one of the fountains."

# 22

## Paradise Found

### Joan Snyder and Maggie Cammer in Park Slope, Brooklyn

MAY 16, 2010

Joan Snyder, the painter, and Maggie Cammer, a retired judge, in their renovated farmhouse in Park Slope, Brooklyn. (Ruth Fremson/*The New York Times*)

THE artist Joan Snyder has lived in many places in her 70 years. Her childhood home was a two-family house in Highland Park, New Jersey, where she grew up the unhappy and anxious daughter of lower-middle-class parents. "My father sold toys to candy stores, and my mother worked for children's clothing stores," Ms. Snyder, the middle of three children, once told an interviewer. "Our parents paid no attention to our emotional life. From the age of 2, I was always looking for another mother."

The list of her subsequent residences includes a farm in Pennsylvania, where she lived with her former husband, the photographer Larry Fink; a loft on Mulberry Street; an old farmhouse on eastern Long Island (with her daughter, Molly Snyder-Fink); a summer house in Woodstock, New York; and for more than two decades, a series of residences in brownstone Brooklyn with Maggie Cammer, a former judge and her partner of 23 years.

Houses have also been a continuing theme in Ms. Snyder's art. Early in her career, she produced an expressionistic landscape titled *The Yellow House*, and in the '70s, she began to incorporate childlike drawings of landscapes, houses, and stick figures into her paintings. One beguiling work, titled *Houses*, combines multicolored images of doors, windows, and peaked roofs. "The painting had images of all the houses that I had lived in but one, which was an imagined white stone house," she says. "Larry and I bought a white stone farmhouse in Pennsylvania a year later. That always seemed magical to me."

In Ms. Snyder's mind, houses not only have symbolic value; they're also capable of bringing great happiness. "Ever since I was young," she says, "I always pictured living in a certain sort of house, one with staircases and two floors and lots of rooms. It was always my fantasy to own a house like that." And if ever a place fulfilled such a fantasy, it's the century-old robin's-egg-blue house on 11th Street in Park Slope, where Ms. Snyder and Ms. Cammer have lived for the past decade.

The two-story building, a frame structure that began life as a farmhouse, has a graceful front porch supported by slender white Doric columns and is wreathed with greenery. The low-slung wooden building in back originally served as a carriage house. Thanks partly to the fishpond in the rear garden, a real estate ad described the property as "paradise found." The place looked more appropriate to a village in New England than the heart of urban Brooklyn.

When the couple discovered the house in 1998, they were living in a nearby brownstone and had been searching for years for a home that included space for a studio. "But as it turned out, a sculptor was also looking at the house," Ms. Cammer recalls, "and a week later we were told that the house was already in contract."

One evening when Ms. Snyder was in New Mexico, Ms. Cammer paid a visit to the broker's office. "I can't get that house on 11th Street out of my mind," Ms. Cammer told the broker, ignoring the fact that neither she nor Ms. Snyder had ever set foot inside and that someone else was taking steps to buy the property. "If anything happens and it becomes available, let me know."

The next night Ms. Cammer got a phone call from the broker, informing her that the deal had fallen through. At 9 the following morning, she showed up at the house with Andrew Mockler, a publisher of Ms. Snyder's prints, to help her conduct a lightning-fast inspection, since the contract had to be signed that day and there wasn't time to hire a home inspector. The story is a family favorite. As Ms. Snyder likes to sum up what happened, "Maggie bought a house when I was in New Mexico."

The couple purchased the two buildings for about $400,000. There followed a gut renovation of the main house, an undertaking that cost $250,000 and involved the removal of nearly 20 Dumpsters' worth of trash. Today it's impossible to picture what the place looked like in its earlier incarnation. Small dark spaces have been opened up to create an airy layout. Greenery is visible from every window. Although Ms. Snyder is the artist in the family, the reconfiguration of the interior was largely the work of Ms. Cammer—"because she's good at space and has a sense of balance," her partner says—and off the master bedroom is one of her most inspired touches, a balcony overlooking the pond where the couple can sit and look at the moon.

Interior design may not be Ms. Cammer's only artistic strong suit. Although she retired as a New York State Acting Supreme Court Justice, she works part-time as a judicial hearing officer and has served as a technical adviser to the television series *Law & Order*. It's disappointing to learn that she didn't perform in front of the camera as well; with her ebullient manner, she would have made a terrifically engaging TV judge.

Ms. Snyder's works have been praised for their expressive, personal, and openly feminist qualities, and her large and lusciously textured paintings dominate these rooms. The sunroom is brightened by a swirl of green and orange called *Sweet Golden Clime* (the title comes from a Blake poem). In the master bedroom hangs *120 Roses for Maggie*, a sumptuous image flecked with rosebuds dipped in glue and painted that was a gift to Ms. Cammer for her 60th birthday.

Ms. Snyder's paintings are kept company by works of many other artists, a number of them friends, including a Louise Bourgeois etching titled *Womanhouse* and a Nancy Spero print bearing the inscription "Love to Joan." The presence of long-gone relatives also hovers over these rooms. An ivory and ebony chess set with a Don Quixote theme (the rooks are miniature windmills) is an inheritance from Ms. Cammer's father, who collected chess sets. In the master bedroom hangs a portrait of a melancholy-looking young Russian with a full beard. The man, Itzhak Saltzman, was Ms. Snyder's great-grandfather, and the portrait hung over her grandmother's bed for her entire life.

The attic contains what Ms. Snyder describes as a "surprise room," an aerie with a steeply angled ceiling where her daughter, now 30, lived for a year with her future husband, Orlando Richards, after the attacks of September 11. By the greatest of coincidences, just the previous day, September 10, Ms. Cammer had helped move Molly to the couple's Park Slope home from an apartment in Williamsburg. The presence of Ms. Snyder-Fink, "surely the most fabulous daughter in all the world," as Ms. Snyder described her in a catalogue essay, is felt throughout the house. Three of her works on paper can be found in the sunroom, for example; two were birthday presents to her mother ("I love you with all my heart," one says), and the third was a birthday present to Ms. Cammer, over more than two decades a second mother to Ms. Snyder-Fink.

The interior of the house is immensely welcoming. Yet in many ways the true heart of the house lies just outside the front door. In the yard facing the street, flowers poke out from behind an iron fence built by an iron sculptor and organic farmer named Tovey Halleck, who used material from a recycled fire escape that he had found in the Brooklyn Navy Yard. In the back, the leafy canopy of a rare Camperdown elm casts shadows on the surface of the koi pond, which is framed by rocks and moss and is home to 18 white and golden fish. Season by season, the garden explodes with color—orange tulips, daffodils, Japanese lilies, a neighbor's magnolia tree, and two butterfly bushes "that do indeed bring butterflies," says Ms. Snyder, clearly impressed that the bushes live up to their reputation. She calls this retreat a little wonderland.

The onetime carriage house has been transformed into a 750-square-foot studio whose 20-foot beamed ceiling is punctuated with skylights. These days, an immense work-in-progress flecked with berries and scraps of burlap hangs on the long wall. Tubes of oil paint and jars of well-worn brushes have the dignity of still lifes. It's hard to imagine a more inviting workplace for an artist.

This isn't Ms. Snyder's only retreat. She also has a commodious studio in Woodstock, where the couple spend the summer. But she feels blessed to return again and again to this space. "I'm immensely lucky," she says. "When I come back from Woodstock, I still feel as if I'm in the country. It's so special, really fabulous in every respect. When I'm here, I feel as if I'm away from time."

# 23

## Trim Jim Creates a Masterpiece

### Anne Landsman, James Wagman, and Their Children on the Upper West Side

DECEMBER 27, 2009

Anne Landsman, a writer, and her architect husband, James Wagman, with their children in their Upper West Side townhouse. (Cathy Orlinski for *The New York Times*)

I N Anne Landsman's latest novel, *The Rowing Lesson*, the writer brings alive her native South Africa in all its glory and despair. She helps the reader picture the Touw River, "folding itself between the ancient stinkwoods and yellowwoods dripping with moss," and describes with quick, vivid strokes the creatures of this remote and exotic world, "the monkeys screaming above your heads" and "the rarest bird of all, the Knysna loerie, with its brilliant blue body and green head."

The Upper West Side of Manhattan, with its stolid apartment houses and cheek-by-jowl brownstones, couldn't seem more distant from this lush landscape, both physically and spiritually. Yet in the limestone town house on West 99th Street where Ms. Landsman lives with her husband, James Wagman, a Philadelphia-born architect, and their children, Tess and Adam, echoes of her homeland reverberate in every corner.

Creatures made of unlikely materials stare grimly down from bookcases and grin crazily from tabletops: chickens clad in ruffled crayon-colored plastic, diminutive pigs and elephants wearing tiny beads, a warthog and a chameleon crafted from scraps of metal, a sable antelope constructed from discarded soda cans. A witch doctor throwing bones gazes balefully from an embroidered pillow. If you were served tea by the couple, the dining room would be redolent with the earthy aroma of rooibos tea, bought from the South African foods section at Fairway. At dinner, the wine would probably be a South African vintage, carted up from the wine fridge in the basement.

On the mantel over the fireplace in Ms. Landsman's top-floor study hangs a metal plaque bearing the words "Dr. G. B. Landsman," a sign that was affixed to the garden wall of her childhood home and is a tangible memory of her late father, the country doctor who inspired the dying character at the heart of *The Rowing Lesson*. *The Practical Home Physician*, the ancient leather-bound volume on a shelf above her desk, was also his. "I left South Africa almost 30 years ago," says Ms. Landsman, whose voice carries unmistakable echoes of her native land. "But I've never left in the world of my imagination."

The couple's house was constructed in 1892, one of eight sister town houses along 99th Street west of Broadway that were the work of the same builder and had been made for a wood importer and his extended family. Though the couple's house started life as a single-family home, during the Depression it was chopped into individual

apartments, and over time both interior and exterior declined. Alcoholics and drug addicts dozed beneath the cherry tree in the front garden, so much so that when the couple were renovating the property, a
worker called it the drinking tree. Photographs taken during the early
stages of construction make it impossible to picture anyone living on
the premises. "It was a complete dump," Ms. Landsman says. "Most
people would have found it totally unappealing. Unless you were married to an architect, you'd never have wanted to undertake a project of
this magnitude."

Ms. Landsman and Mr. Wagman met in 1988, when they were both
in their late 20s, and were drawn together in part by their mutual admiration for Frank Lloyd Wright, admiration so deep that they were married in the celebrated Wright synagogue in Elkins Park, Pennsylvania.
In 1997, when they discovered the house on 99th Street, they and their
daughter, then 2, were living in a loft near the Bowery, in a neighborhood
so rough that the couple had their own rat in residence.

They bought the house the following year, paying $825,000, and
through laborious surgery that ultimately cost nearly as much as the purchase price, they coaxed the building back to life. But renovations took
more than a year, and when the family finally moved in, the work was far
from finished.

Even someone unfamiliar with the history of the house would be impressed by its sleek and generous spaces. But the more you know about
its past, the more you appreciate its glowing present. The warren of tiny
disorganized spaces was reconfigured to create rooms that flow into one
another. And though all the detailing looks indigenous to the house, that
is not the case. "Two of the sister town houses were scheduled to be demolished to make way for a high-rise," Mr. Wagman explains, "and they
let me go in so I could salvage various items that I needed." Mr. Wagman,
or Trim Jim, as Ms. Landsman likes to call her husband in an affectionate tip of the hat to his obsession with molding and the like, can escort
a visitor through the four floors of rooms and point out all the elements
that came from somewhere else. His finds included the carved rosettes
on some of the interior doors and the wood trim around the half-dozen
fireplaces edged respectively with mouth-watering green, pink, and beige
ceramic tile. The rooms also showcase an eclectic assortment of artwork,
not only images that momentarily transport Ms. Landsman back to her
homeland but also inheritances from the house where Mr. Wagman grew
up, notably an oil of two solemn-eyed children by a 19th-century Philadelphian named John Carlin.

Though a modest 14 feet wide, the house is studded with elegant touches, among them high ceilings, skylights, stained glass, sliding doors, and a French crystal chandelier from Mr. Wagman's childhood home that illuminates the expanses of cherry and white oak, the two main woods used in the interior. The men who once dozed beneath the cherry tree are long gone, and in the spring a cloud of pink blossoms is visible from tall windows that face the street. The backyard, shadowed by the new high-rise, is as compact as a Lego construction.

Like so many of the city's impeccably restored town houses, the couple's home looks as well appointed as a stage set. But the exquisite details did not arrive without domestic drama. "James likes to renovate," Ms. Landsman explains. "I like it when the renovation is done. Being a writer, I don't like things moved." She explores some of the issues involved in creating a home with another person in an essay titled "White Knight," published in a collection of works about the stresses that can tear at even the most blissful relationships. In this piece, she mulls her decision to marry an architect instead of a doctor like her father, to share her life with someone "who can barely distinguish a virus from a bacteria, grippe from coup, staph from strep."

"His world is the world of aesthetics, measurements, details," Ms. Landsman continues. "He is passionate about green design, finding the right wood stain, the right white, the most beautiful ceiling fan, light fixture, doorknob. He loves doing origami, and our home is full of paper stars, cranes, frogs, polyhedrons." As for the spaces they dreamed of inhabiting, "I know there is a gray gardens lurking somewhere in my soul, a wish to leave everything in my immediate presence in the same hallowed spot for the next 40 or so years, so I know exactly where it is." Her husband, by contrast, dreamed of a "glistening, spotlessly clean modernist castle, true to the principles he learned from his teachers at architecture school."

These conflicting worldviews expressed themselves in the beginning of their marriage, when the couple renovated a loft, and flared up again when the time came to restore the town house. One memorable battle was waged over the color of the interior woodwork. Trim Jim, who's indeed nothing if not obsessive about such matters, found it too dark and was so upset that portions of the woodwork eventually had to be redone. But what Ms. Landsman describes as the worst fight of their marriage involved what shade of white to paint the stairway. "My white, Pearly Gates, was a soft white, with yellow undertones, a hint of tea stain and parchment," she writes. "His white, Downy Gray, had cool blue undertones. My white was an old white; his white was a new white. Never had we fought harder than we did over those shades of difference."

The solution was a compromise, but an elegant compromise. "I remember watching one of the painters pouring Pearly Gates into the bucket of Downy Gray," Ms. Landsman writes, "and mixing the two colors with a stick."

# Old Stomping Grounds

# 24

## Ensconced in the Bronx

José Diaz-Oyola on the Grand Concourse in the Bronx

JULY 19, 2009

José Diaz-Oyola, a health care worker from Puerto Rico, in his Art Deco apartment on the Grand Concourse in the Bronx. (Michelle V. Agins/*The New York Times*)

O N a frigid January day in 1975, two years before the sportscaster Howard Cosell used the occasion of a World Series game at Yankee Stadium to inform the nation that the Bronx was burning, a 29-year-old nurse named José Diaz-Oyola moved into a two-bedroom apartment on the Grand Concourse.

Mr. Diaz-Oyola had been born in Puerto Rico, one of 13 children. His father came to the United States to work in the Ohio steel mills, and his mother followed a few years later. By 1966, Mr. Diaz-Oyola had made his way to New York, where he lived for a time with a sister in the South Bronx. When she left the city, he moved to this apartment and for $315 a month acquired a foothold in an Art Deco building on what was once the most beautiful street in the borough.

Mr. Diaz-Oyola's story offers a window onto the rise, fall, and shaky rebirth of the Grand Concourse, one of the great urban dramas of the 20th century. The four-and-a-half-mile-long tree-lined thoroughfare, which celebrates its centennial this year, was for decades a prime destination for the city's upwardly mobile Jews. For these strivers, many of whom were children of immigrants, an address on or even near the boulevard carried immeasurable cachet, as did residence in one of the handsome Art Deco apartment houses that lined its flanks.

But starting in the 1960s, and continuing with increasing vigor in the 1970s and into the '80s, this once solid and nurturing world began crumbling under the weight of poverty and neglect. The blight ravaging the South Bronx lapped ferociously at its edges, bringing crime, drugs, fires, building abandonment, social chaos, and most of all, a sense of a metropolis spun out of control. The street that had been home to the elegant Concourse Plaza Hotel, with its velvet banquettes and crystal chandeliers, and the fabled Loew's Paradise, a movie theater where stars twinkled in a cinematic heaven, grew shabby, then dangerous. Seemingly overnight, a white middle-class population was replaced by low-income blacks and Hispanics, large numbers of whom were on welfare, and as much victims of this crumbling world as those who had come before.

Public and private institutions were powerless to staunch the bleeding. And while the Bronx's troubles were hardly unique, while cities across the nation collapsed like dominos in those years, here the devastation was so swift and brutal that the term "South Bronx" became code for the worst of urban decay. It's no wonder Cosell's words at Yankee Stadium resonated decades after he had uttered them.

The Grand Concourse and the neighborhoods on its fringes suffered mightily in those years. But the apartment houses along the boulevard escaped many of the ravages, and much of their beauty remains intact. If you walk down the boulevard today, you can still see the glittering mosaics on the façade of the Fish Building, the luscious murals illustrating a Joyce Kilmer poem just inside No. 910, and the lobby of No. 888, with its sultry curves—all reminders of an era of grace and prosperity. In the lobby of Mr. Diaz-Oyola's building, a red and green terrazzo floor peeks out from beneath the carpet. The silvery elevators are original except for their buttons.

Most of the people who witnessed the boulevard's transformation disappeared decades ago. Nearly all the longtime white residents moved away, and many of them are no longer alive. The blacks and Hispanics who swept into the apartments they had left behind were largely transient, and most of them are gone, too. But 34 years after Mr. Diaz-Oyola arrived, his rent having inched up to a still manageable $1,100, he is still happily ensconced in his seventh-floor apartment. As someone who observed the changes along the boulevard firsthand, he's a living witness to both the bleak times and the more cheerful ones that followed as crime and drugs eased their grip on the city and once-desolate neighborhoods became increasingly desirable. In a place whose history was forged by immigrants and their offspring, Mr. Diaz-Oyola represents an essential strand of the story.

When he arrived, he was the only Hispanic in the building, and at first he remained more through inertia than anything else. "In the beginning," says Mr. Diaz-Oyola, a balding, solidly built man with a neat mustache and a white goatee, "I stayed mainly because I just hate to move." But he developed an affection for his neighbors, many of them elderly Jews who were holding on despite the ground shifting beneath their feet. He particularly remembers the couple who lived next door. The husband had Alzheimer's disease, and when he wandered the halls naked, Mr. Diaz-Oyola used to wrap him in a blanket and return him to his wife.

Over time, Mr. Diaz-Oyola also became attached to the neighborhood. He joined the community board, became chairman of its parks committee, and is especially proud of the committee's role on behalf of the Lorelei Fountain, a century-old marble concoction in Joyce Kilmer Park depicting the siren who lured sailors to their death with her singing and her beauty. The statue, which Mr. Diaz-Oyola can see from his window, had been vandalized in the 1970s and '80s and was poised to be relocated to a less tumultuous neighborhood where, proponents of this plan contended, residents would take better care of it. "My stance was that the fountain stays in this community," Mr. Diaz-Oyola says. It did, and he, like Lorelei, seems rooted here as well, proud to play a role in the boulevard's continuing fortunes. "Today," he says, "I wouldn't live anywhere else."

Although early on Mr. Diaz-Oyola had a roommate, a childhood friend who was among the first victims of AIDS, ever since 1987 he has lived in this apartment by himself. Not having to cater to someone else's tastes has allowed him to put his own stamp on the space, a stamp that begins at the front door.

The moment you enter the foyer you're greeted by dozens of grinning or grimacing faces. These are masks from around the world—Puerto Rico, Venice, St. Petersburg, Mexico, Brazil, Costa Rica—that were acquired by Mr. Diaz-Oyola on his travels or given to him by friends on theirs. Go down the two steps, edged with a little wrought-iron railing, and you're in the sunken living room that was a beloved fixture of the Art Deco apartment houses along the boulevard. So were the wraparound casement windows, through which for decades, until the new stadium was built, Mr. Diaz-Oyola could see in the distance the place where Cosell uttered his sadly memorable words. The floors are parquet, with a different design in each room.

Streets once lined with garbage and drug paraphernalia yielded treasures. From a long-defunct hospital in the South Bronx, Mr. Diaz-Oyola salvaged a Singer sewing machine table that he converted into a bar. He rescued the pitted stone head atop the remains of a column after a fire at his local subway station.

The luxuriant bamboo plant that stands in the small jungle of greenery at the front window also comes with a story. Mr. Diaz-Oyola works for a social services agency that serves the chronically ill, and the bamboo had been owned by one of his patients. Mr. Diaz-Oyola had always admired the plant, and after the patient died, his widow arranged to have it delivered to Mr. Diaz-Oyola's apartment.

Although Mr. Diaz-Oyola's family is scattered, their presence is felt in these rooms. A half century's worth of photographs of relatives and his five godchildren plaster a wall in his bedroom. A cabinet in the foyer that holds more than a dozen costumed dolls—from Greece, Spain, Korea, and Latin America—stands as a shrine to his late mother. "This was her collection," Mr. Diaz-Oyola says of the exquisitely gowned little creatures outfitted in a rainbow array of silks and satins. "I used to say to her, 'Mom, when I grow up, the only thing I want when you die is your dolls.'" He talks about what his mother's life must have been like, tending to such a large brood in a place so far from where she was born. "She was 91 when she died," he says. "She was a tough old bird, managing with all those children. She didn't have an easy time."

The apartment may be shadowed by relics from Mr. Diaz-Oyola's past. But once a year, the day of his annual Christmas party, the place is rooted in the present. A giant tree presides in his living room, wreaths line his walls and spill out into the hallway, and 150, maybe 200 people show up. There's dancing in the foyer, and Mr. Diaz-Oyola cooks up a storm in his pocket-size kitchen, including what he describes as some mean collard greens. He serves a potent punch called Sex on the Beach that includes vodka and peach schnapps. "My friends," he says, "call it the social event of the year." Ironically, the only occasion Mr. Diaz-Oyola was ever a victim of a crime, in a neighborhood that has seen far more than its share, occurred at one of these bashes. Someone—he has no idea who—made off with a large mantle clock.

# 25

## Over the Family Store, Staff Quarters

### Mary Gannett and Her Sons in Cobble Hill, Brooklyn

JULY 26, 2009

Mary Gannett in her apartment above the family bookstore in Cobble Hill, Brooklyn. (Chester Higgins Jr./*The New York Times*)

THE story of the family that lives above BookCourt, a much-loved independent bookstore in Cobble Hill, Brooklyn, begins in 1979 in the venerable WordsWorth Books in Cambridge, Massachusetts. The staff included a pair of part-timers in their early 20s named Henry Zook and Mary Gannett, and in a "maybe someday" kind of way, they thought about opening a bookstore of their own. A photograph posted decades later on Facebook captures them as they looked in those years—he with a mop of fuzzy hair, she an angelic blonde, and both seeming incredibly young.

By 1980, the two were married, working for New York publishing houses, and living on Cheever Place in Cobble Hill, an appropriately named address for such a bookish pair. The following year, the couple rented the ground floor of a pre–Civil War frame house at 163 Court Street. Where Dom's Barbershop had sat for a quarter of a century, they opened their own little bookstore, a place with much of the intimacy and ambience of the one where they had met. Nor did they stop there. In 1984, shortly after the birth of their first son, Zachary, the couple bought the entire building for $160,000, and within two years the family was installed in the duplex above the store.

The son—Zack to everyone except his mother—claims he can remember the day they moved in. He definitely remembers the years that followed. "It was a great house to grow up in," Zack says as he lounges on a bench outside the store, dressed this day in rolled-up chinos and a Flaming Lips T-shirt. He and a friend used to jump over the fences that separated his family's back garden from the gardens on either side. When he was very young, he would look out the front window facing Court Street and hold his breath until someone passed. Cobble Hill was a far quieter neighborhood in those days, and sometimes the street was so empty, he couldn't quite make it.

By 1990, with the birth of a second child, Benjamin, there were four of them in the duplex, along with assorted pets. (An early store cat named Zoe was exiled from the premises after lunging at a fish in a customer's shopping bag; this was back when Cobble Hill was home to many Italian families, and the ill-fated fish had been intended for someone's Christmas Eve dinner.) The year Benjamin was born, the couple expanded into the building's dirt basement; Ms. Gannett still winces at the memory of a major renovation conducted with an infant in residence.

Six years later, the couple spent $700,000 to acquire the brick build-
ing next door at 161 Court Street, the storefront of which had been the
home of Albert's Floral Shop and is locally celebrated for its star turn in
the movie *Moonstruck*.

All this additional space allowed Ms. Gannett and Mr. Zook to signifi-
cantly expand the store, which is now more than five times its original
size. What Zack remembered as a "creepy greenhouse," complete with a
giant turtle, has made way for a sky-lighted expanse where readings are
held. Other changes over the years included the arrival of a Barnes &
Noble a few blocks away in 1999 and the couple's separation in 2002.
Yet today, most of the family still lives above the store. Ms. Gannett, who
handles the shop's finances and is the children's-book buyer, lives upstairs
in No. 163 with Ben. Zack, the general manager, is ensconced on the top
floor of No. 161. Mr. Zook, the senior buyer, lives nearby on Douglass
Street. "We converge every day at the store," Zack says. "It's psychotic,
but it works."

Longtime costumers who know and are fond of both Ms. Gannett and
Mr. Zook sometimes think to themselves that such an arrangement must
have its painful moments. But they forget how much BookCourt means
to both of them. "In a way," Ms. Gannett says, "the store was like our
first child. That was the part that was working; about that, we were of
the same mind-set. Neither of us wanted to give it up."

Even as New York becomes a city of chains and megastores, as mom-
and-pop operations struggle to stay afloat, small businesses like Book-
Court survive and prosper. Many do so because the proprietor was savvy
enough to buy the building where the business is located. And, like Ms.
Gannett, some of these proprietors live right over the store—"just like
the Obamas," as Ms. Gannett likes to describe her situation.

For the family, the arrangement made for a seamlessly integrated life,
one in which their personal and professional selves were intertwined.
Once in a while customers complained about hearing Ben bounce his bas-
ketball above their heads. But that was rare. Many more people waved
to Ms. Gannett when they saw her in her second-floor office above the
original shop, as if cosmopolitan Brooklyn were some Mayberry-like
small town. They saw her in the neighborhood, hurrying to the grocery
store or rushing back from the gym. And for the children there was always one great upside. Both boys, and especially Zack, were intimately
familiar with the rhythms of the store and their parents' professional
selves. As their mother sums it up, "Our kids always knew what we did
for a living."

The building where the family has lived for most of the past 25 years is a graceful structure whose windows and front door are edged in sage green, a color chosen, Ms. Gannett says, "with New England in mind." Early on, elderly Italian-American women who remembered the funeral parlor that preceded the barbershop used to cross themselves when they passed. And the duplex retains much of its original charm; anyone with a taste for 19th-century domestic architecture would melt in the presence of the painted tin ceilings, the soft pine floors, the marble fireplaces. Although closets were added and the kitchen renovated, it's easy to picture the lives lived in these rooms a century and a half ago.

Even relatively modern inheritances come with provenances. The gold-leaf mirror was rescued from the barbershop. The upright piano came from Andy Warhol's Factory and was once played by Lou Reed, or so the previous tenants, who left behind the piano, insist. The claw-foot oak table in the living room, which can seat a dozen with the three leaves in, came from a summer bungalow. From Ms. Gannett's mother came a collection called *My Bookhouse*, a set of children's stories from the 1920s that used to be sold door to door. Mary's childhood rocker, black with gold stenciling, is here, along with a portrait of Mr. Zook as a dreamy boy. In his face, Ms. Gannett says she sees the face of her younger son.

A china cabinet holds an old family tureen along with pitchers and teapots, many of them blue and white, Ms. Gannett's favorite colors, and relics of what she describes as "a more gracious age," though these rooms hardly lack graciousness. The plates with an Art Deco floral pattern that hang on a wall near the kitchen were passed down from her maternal grandmother, who died when Ms. Gannett's mother was 7 and after whom Ms. Gannett was named. The Meissen plates in the Blue Onion pattern were a gift from Ms. Gannett's mother-in-law, who, she says, "shared my blue and white passion." From the kitchen window, you can see the slightly scruffy garden, which includes a crabapple tree from Mr. Zook's mother and a plant that once sat in the window of India House, a local restaurant. "We learned they were closing," Ms. Gannett recalls. "So we said to them, 'It's so sad you're leaving, but can we have a plant?'"

The third floor is very different in tone, at least when it comes to Ben's bedroom, where bright orange and yellow walls are plastered with exuberant scrawls and scribblings. And thanks to the small doorway between the buildings, Zack is down the hall, ensconced on the top floor of No. 161, a pale-green brick building with nearly as much charm as its next-door neighbor.

The décor in Zack's room includes a red-painted tin ceiling ("Very funky at night," he reports), a brick fireplace, and soft pine floors just like the floors he grew up with. The window faces a broad swath of Brooklyn that includes the tennis bubble of a branch of the New York Sports Club. "Pretty cool, right?" he says.

His mother finds the whole arrangement extremely cool. "Zachary is still at home," she says. "It's like the old extended family."

# 26

# With Sky and the Weather for Neighbors

## Barbara McCall and Her Family in Soundview, the Bronx

AUGUST 30, 2009

Barbara McCall with her daughter and grandson in their apartment in Soundview in the Bronx. (Rob Bennett for *The New York Times*)

FROM Barbara McCall's 22nd-floor apartment in the Soundview section of the Bronx, she can see the world.

From her living room window, she can take in the entire sweep of the Manhattan skyline, including the Empire State Building, where her daughter, Scherrie, works as a dental assistant. She can see three bridges—the George Washington, the Throgs Neck, and the Whitestone—along with the East River, Long Island Sound, and the Jersey Palisades. From her daughter's bedroom, she can watch as planes land and take off from Kennedy and LaGuardia airports and sometimes circle endlessly, up to half a dozen at a time. In a tower somewhere, air traffic controllers are presumably chewing their nails, but Ms. McCall couldn't be more entranced. "It's interesting when the skies get crowded," she says.

Most spectacularly, she can watch the Macy's Fourth of July fireworks while listening to the musical accompaniment on television. "Every year when they have the fireworks, I look forward to it," she says. "I don't have to go downtown. I can sit in my bedroom and look from the TV to what's really happening." Television, she acknowledges, doesn't begin to capture the beauty.

Ms. McCall, a retired nurse with a round face and a halo of curly dark hair, has lived in this building for over 40 years, nearly all of them in this three-bedroom apartment, which she shares with her daughter, her 9-year-old grandson, Marques, four cats, and a Shih Tzu named Thaddeus.

Serendipity brought her here. Born in South Carolina in 1943, she moved to New York with her family the following year, grew up in Washington Heights, and in 1963 married a New York police officer named Tommy McCall. The photographs in this apartment suggest that Tommy must have been a heartbreaker, or as she says of their relationship, "Those eyes got me into trouble." At 19, the couple decided to elope, but when they headed to Maryland to tie the knot—they had heard that the state was lenient in such matters—the would-be bridegroom was sent back home because he didn't have his parents' permission, and they had to return the following week.

For four years, the McCalls lived in a tiny two-bedroom apartment on Nelson Avenue in the West Bronx. But Officer McCall had his father's car, in which the couple used to explore other parts of town—the Polo Grounds, the local White Castle—and on one such drive they discovered the Leland Houses, a pair of green-brick towers on Thieriot Avenue near the Bruckner Expressway. The complex had been constructed under the city's Mitchell-Lama program, which keeps rents affordable for moderate-income families, and in 1967, two days before Christmas, the couple moved into a two-bedroom apartment for which the rent was just over $100. "We were paying $81 on Nelson Avenue," Ms. McCall recalls. "We were a little nervous about paying the rent here."

A few years later, with a young son and daughter in residence, the McCalls moved to the three-bedroom apartment next door; the building manager who approved the arrangement had a soft spot in his heart for cops. The rent, originally about $300, is now about $1,150, and though the building is no longer part of the Mitchell-Lama program, costs are still kept modest.

Ms. McCall, whose husband died in 2003 from injuries suffered in a fall, hasn't had an easy life. In the late 1970s, she went back to school to study nursing and eventually ended up as a dialysis nurse at Mount Sinai Hospital. But in 1982 she had a stroke that left her paralyzed for nearly a year, and she regained her mobility only after months of rehabilitation. Even today, she still has stiffness on her left side and is slowed by arthritis in her knees and hips. She also has diabetes, and from the gingerly way she moves about the apartment, it's obvious that she has trouble getting around.

Nor is the apartment fancy. Thanks to the ravages of the cats, foam peeks out of some of the sofa cushions. A washer and dryer occupy one corner of the living room, not far from the cage where Thaddeus is fed so the cats don't steal his food. The terrace off the living room is so small that there's barely room to stick a toe outside. For a brief time, Ms. McCall and her daughter carpeted the terrace with AstroTurf, and they once tried to grow tomatoes. Both experiments were abandoned, and today all that's left are a few scraggly pots of herbs.

The neighborhood is home to eight public housing projects, and while crime and poverty in Soundview have declined as they have through much of the city, many residents are poor and many streets are still rough. It was in Soundview, in 1999, that a 23-year-old Guinean immigrant named Amadou Diallo was fatally shot outside his building by four cops who were pursuing a serial rapist who himself lived in the neighborhood. Diallo's name, which became an instant code word for senseless police violence, will forever be associated with this section of the city.

Yet in a sense there are two Soundviews, with Story Avenue, which runs below the Bruckner and bisects the neighborhood, serving as a dividing line. The southern portion, where the McCalls live, is the more stable section, home to many working families with children. Scherrie McCall remembers the streets of her childhood as quiet and residential and her immediate area as largely untroubled by urban ills. As is often the case in a city as complicated as New York, there's a disconnect between the broad-brush image of a neighborhood painted by government statistics and police reports and the experiences of people who inhabit the neighborhood's more tranquil portions, who shop at local supermarkets, and whose children attend local schools and play in local parks.

As for Barbara McCall, she simply says, "I'm spoiled"—and not just because of the amazing views or a night sky that she describes as "gorgeous, just gorgeous." She's quick to tick off the other advantages, not only the reasonable rent but also the convenient shopping, a sense of safety within her complex, and the parking lot outside her door. From her window, she can see her grandson's elementary school, the same one her daughter attended decades earlier. "I can't imagine what an apartment like this would cost downtown," Ms. McCall says. "We have 24-hour security. We don't have to worry about parking because we have an assigned space." In a car, she can be in Manhattan in 12 minutes.

Getting to Manhattan easily is something Ms. McCall prizes because of her involvement in Trinity Baptist Church, housed in a handsome building on East 61st Street. "When I accepted the Lord," she says in response to the inevitable question, which is why does she worship so far from home, "I asked for a church. They gave me a list, and I fell in love with Trinity." She describes herself as the church's chief cook—"that's my ministry"—and the job keeps her busy. "You know Christians love to eat," she says. "Plus we have lots of functions."

As to any downsides of her home in the clouds, Ms. McCall must think for a minute. One of the few drawbacks is that she sometimes feels too close to the weather. She recalls a recent rainstorm when hailstones pelted the terrace so intensely, she feared the worst was about to happen. "It was a little unnerving," says Ms. McCall, who couldn't help but remember dramatic Weather Channel accounts of hail followed by tornadoes. Was a tornado poised to hit the Bronx that day? "I didn't know," she admits. "But like I say, when you hear the train coming, cancel Christmas."

# 27

# A Hand-Me-Down Home

## Kim Stolz on the Upper East Side

OCTOBER 11, 2009

Kim Stolz, a contestant on *America's Next Top Model*, in her Upper East Side penthouse. (Fred Conrad/*The New York Times*)

KIM STOLZ lives in an apartment that embodies the geography of her childhood. It was in this two-bedroom aerie on East 84th Street—her father's bachelor pad turned family home—that Ms. Stolz used to slide across the parquet floor in her socks when she was 5. It was in this living room that she gazed into the angled mirrors on the walls and saw her reflection repeated as far as the eye could see, a disconcerting experience for an only child. And it was at the age of 16, standing by the living room couch, that Ms. Stolz informed her parents that she was gay. It was, she recalls, sitting just feet from where she stood on that occasion, the most emotional experience of her young life.

Ms. Stolz, the 26-year-old daughter of a stockbroker (Goldman Sachs) and a supermodel (Carol Brandt, who modeled for Givenchy and Ralph Lauren), is a member of an exclusive club of New Yorkers, those who long after reaching adulthood live in the place where they grew up. The arrangement offers mixed blessings. On the one hand, remaining in such a setting can do a great deal to reawaken the traumas of childhood. The moments of misery inevitable in those years can seem embedded in the walls, the floorboards, the views out the windows. Yet a person lucky enough to inhabit a family apartment generally lives far better and—no small matter in pricy New York—far more reasonably than would otherwise be possible.

Ms. Stolz, one of a handful of New Yorkers who live in such a space, had an utterly typical Upper East Side childhood: she attended Madison Avenue Presbyterian Nursery School, followed by the Brearley School from kindergarten through 12th grade. The month she graduated from high school, her parents moved to London, making the family apartment her de facto home during her years at Wesleyan, where she majored in government.

Now, after a brief interlude in a one-bedroom in Prospect Heights, Brooklyn, an apartment defined by the presence of cockroaches and the absence of air-conditioning, Ms. Stolz is back in the 21-story white brick building where she has spent nearly her entire life. The apartment stayed in the family thanks to the miracle of rent stabilization, under which certain rents remain low as long as the tenant's income stays below a specified level for a specified period of time. The 1,500-square-foot penthouse, for which Ms. Stolz pays about $2,100 a month, is now legally hers, turned over to her by her parents.

Ms. Stolz always assumed that after college she would go to law school or work in the field of foreign policy. Instead, after losing a bet with a friend, she went to an *America's Next Top Model* audition, where her green eyes and lustrous dark hair helped her come in fifth in Season 5, which was broadcast in 2005. After her stint on the show, she worked for a time as a model, but now she's eager to get back onto her original track. Her college major, along with a job as a paralegal at a law firm, whetted her appetite for more serious pursuits. She's applying to law school and at the same time working on a book about the impact on her generation of Twitter, television, and social networking sites.

In terms of furnishings and décor, much in the apartment has altered since she was young. The grand piano she played as a child is gone, as is the old television set, replaced by a 47-inch flat-screen TV, as befits a tenant whose résumé includes stints as a correspondent for MTV News. Other additions include a poster for *Top Model* and, in her bedroom, formerly her parents', a $150 armoire from Housing Works that has seen better days. But the sweeping view from the living room windows, which face south and overlook a broad swath of Midtown, is as sparkling as ever, especially after dark. The rug in the foyer is the one Ms. Stolz remembers from her childhood. The majesty palm has presided in a corner of the living room ever since her father arrived here as a bachelor in 1978.

A vintage Duel turntable that belonged to her grandfather survives, and the all-white galley kitchen is so unchanged that when Ms. Stolz hears her cell phone ring, she sometimes reaches for a telephone receiver, forgetting that the land line of her childhood is long since a memory. The kitchen is a time capsule in another way. Taped to the wall are two photographs, one of Ms. Stolz as a solemn-eyed girl wearing a dress with a huge white collar, the other of her mother in full supermodel regalia. Also unchanged is the presence in her life of a trio of women from South America—Celina and Anacia from Colombia and Teresa from Ecuador—who cleaned the apartment when Ms. Stolz was a child and, except for Teresa, who recently became ill, still do so.

In this place so layered with remnants of the past, déjà vu moments are inevitable and occasionally disconcerting. Once when Ms. Stolz was rooting around in a closet, she found her father's little black book, a survivor from his bachelor days, filled with name after name of available women. Once when she was leaving her apartment, she unthinkingly took the service elevator down to the basement garage, even though the family's car hadn't been parked there for years. When she's cooking, she sometimes assumes that she can step out onto the narrow terrace and pick a handful of basil, even though it has been years since her mother grew pots of herbs there.

Memories furnish this space as surely as the chairs and tables, or as Ms. Stolz says, "I can tell you something that happened in every room." She remembers where she was sitting when she got her first dog, a black and white cocker spaniel named Speckles. She remembers where she was standing when her mother told her Speckles had died. She also remembers, as who doesn't, the ups and downs of her teens. "All hell broke loose for a couple of years," Ms. Stolz says. On occasion, she and her parents got along so poorly that the three of them sat around the dining room table in total silence.

Today, she describes her parents as among her best friends. And she's rapidly accumulating memories of the apartment that are all her own, cheerful ones like the first New Year's Eve party she threw here. Nowadays, she sits in the same spot where those silent dinners took place, studying for her LSATs. "It's a bit strange," Ms. Stolz says. "When I was at Brearley, with all those really rich girls, I was embarrassed to have play dates here because I had one of the smallest apartments. And now I have the biggest house of all my friends."

# 28

# The Leader of the Cheers

### Renee Flowers and Her Son in Boerum Hill, Brooklyn

JANUARY 10, 2010

Renee Flowers, leader of the Gowanus Wildcats Drill Team, in Gowanus Houses in Boerum Hill, Brooklyn. (Chester Higgins Jr./*The New York Times*)

GOWANUS HOUSES, a complex of 14 red-brick buildings in South Brooklyn that sits not far from its namesake canal, opened on a June day in 1949, flush with the optimism that wreathed new housing developments for low-income New Yorkers during the postwar years. Among the 1,100-plus original families was a young couple named Leslie and Victoria Baskett Flowers, married just two years earlier and recently up from the South as part of the Great Migration.

Mr. Flowers worked in a printing firm, and his wife was a welder. Their first apartment had two bedrooms, but they moved into a three-bedroom unit around the time the fourth of their seven children was born in 1954. The first child to be born after they moved to the new apartment was a little girl whom they christened Renee. By the time she was a student at Hunter College, her friends were calling her Juice, thanks to her inexplicable preference for orange juice over more popular items like Coke and Pepsi.

Like many of the "originals," as the project's early residents were called, Leslie and Victoria Flowers are no longer alive. But their daughter, who works in a post office in East New York, still lives in the apartment where she grew up. And a third generation is in residence. The apartment is also home to her 31-year-old son, Darryl, whose father, to whom Ms. Flowers is engaged, is a longtime friend.

Ms. Flowers, who pays about $1,000 in rent, isn't sure how much her parents paid when they arrived, but if she wanted to, she could check because she has saved all the old receipts. "I hardly throw anything away," she admits. "You name it, it's around here somewhere."

Ms. Flowers's half century plus in Gowanus Houses offers a window into the world of the city's public housing and how that world has evolved. Given the terrible press the projects have received through much of their existence—focusing on crime, filth, violence, social disarray—it's nearly impossible to remember what a beacon of hope they represented when they appeared on the scene and how eager young families like the Flowerses were to live in them.

The projects that sprung up after the war were architecturally undistinguished towers characterized by "incredible design mediocrity," as Richard Plunz, a historian of New York City housing, described the prevailing look. But at least in their early years, these complexes were cleaner and safer than the tenements where the bulk of their initial residents had lived. They offered a sense of community and, even more prized, the promise of upward mobility.

As the '50s drifted into the '60s and the projects began their downward slide, this rosy picture faded. First heroin, then crack cocaine helped transform many projects into increasingly terrifying places, especially for the young and the elderly. Crime skyrocketed as the buildings tumbled into neglect. Almost entirely, blacks and Latinos came to dominate these complexes, ensuring that public housing projects would be segregated racially as well as economically.

Though Gowanus Houses didn't lie within such notorious Brooklyn slums as East New York and Bedford-Stuyvesant, the complex hardly escaped blight. Even today, if you Google the words "Gowanus Houses," you see article after article about urban trouble—drug busts, gun violence, senseless killing. (In late 2010, when nine members of a heroin and crack-cocaine ring based at Gowanus Houses were indicted, a United States attorney announced that the arrests disrupted "an alleged prolific drug trafficking crew that operated for years and victimized an entire housing development.")

Ms. Flowers knows about many of these troubles firsthand. Her life has been brushed by the sorrow and disarray that is commonplace in places like Gowanus Houses. In the living room is a reminder of a death close to home, a pillowcase with a silk-screened image of Ms. Flowers's godson, Ta-shon Lee, who was killed across the street from her building when he was 18. Fingering the fabric and gazing out her window, she talks about the night of his murder. "He was shot over some sort of disagreement," she says. "No one really knows what happened. He was a sweetheart of a child."

Even in small ways, Ms. Flowers fights back. A self-described poet who whips up rhymes for virtually any occasion, she recently plastered the hallways of her building with Xeroxed copies of a poem she wrote urging residents to take better care of the elevators, a perennial dumping ground for garbage and worse. "The condition of 'Our Castle' needs to be improved," one line went. "And it's going to be up to us to make a positive move."

Ms. Flowers is also a local celebrity. She is the prime mover behind the Gowanus Wildcats Drill Team, an organization designed to keep the girls of Gowanus House and nearby neighborhoods—"my young ladies," as Ms. Flowers calls them—active and out of trouble. Currently 19 strong and ranging in age from 8 to 22, the Wildcats perform drills that combine stepping, marching, and what Ms. Flowers calls "cheerleading without the pompoms."

From the start, rules were strict. "If you were caught chewing gum, you had to stick it on your nose," Ms. Flowers says. Even though she was just 13 when she took over the Wildcats from another Renee—Renee Turner, who had started the group two years earlier—she continued that rigorous approach. And the drills, sometimes performed to Ms. Flowers's streetwise raps and marching songs with titles like "Crack Is Whack," are strictly G-rated. "If it wasn't ladylike," Ms. Flowers says, "we didn't do it. Nothing on the floor. Nothing grindy. I tell the young ladies, 'Don't even ask.'"

Over the years, she has trained more than 500 girls, a group that includes the daughters of some of the original members. They show off their skills at parades and at places like the Apollo Theater, and they rehearse at public housing community centers, but their de facto headquarters is Ms. Flowers's cluttered living room, with a laundry cart against one wall near her collection of stuffed animals.

Wildcats memorabilia lurks in every corner, starting with a Patti Playpal doll propped up on the sofa and wearing the team's uniform of red pleated skirt, matching tam and T-shirt, and white leather majorette boots adorned with taps and tassels. The uniform has evolved from the hot-purple skirts and gold dashikis that the first Wildcats wore, but the boots, passed down through the years because they were so expensive, have remained unchanged. Ms. Flowers makes the tassels herself, using red and white yarn, just as the other Renee taught her decades earlier.

Ms. Flowers has also compiled dozens of leather-bound scrapbooks, stuffed with photos, programs, and newspaper clippings that document the team's history and occupy an entire wall of her son's bedroom. Propped on tabletops and stashed in corners are team mementos, among them the trophy the Wildcats won when they took first place in the New York City Housing Authority's Talent Search. One photo shows Ms. Flowers in her own Wildcat days, a girl in whose face you can recognize the woman she is today. In another, she holds the giant bronze subway token she received when she was honored by City Lore, an organization that supports urban folk culture.

A calendar that helps Ms. Flowers remember the birthdays of her large extended family—no easy task in a clan with seven siblings who among them have 16 children and 6 grandchildren—is posted on the refrigerator, and her life seems to be documented on these walls. Seven framed color photographs show Ms. Flowers and her brothers and sisters wearing caps, gowns, and broad smiles to celebrate their graduation from high school. Just below these images hang photographs of the next generation, including a nephew, Khalik, who died in a traffic accident at the age of 23. Pictures taken last year show Ms. Flowers and friends celebrating their 50th birthdays—"50 and still hot," as they cheerfully described themselves. Scrapbooks with photos of family reunions and get-togethers date back to the '40s and record an endless round of picnics, pizza parties, and other celebratory events.

Gazing out from a wall in her living room are Ms. Flowers's parents as they looked in 1981, when they had been married for more than 45 years. Mr. Flowers, who would die the following year, wears a brightly patterned shirt and a thin mustache and encircles his wife's waist with his arm. The glare of the camera's flashbulb catches both their faces, below which Ms. Flowers has written an inscription that begins, "They began our strong family tree."

If she wanted to, Ms. Flowers could probably live somewhere else; with a relatively secure government job, she has options. But the idea of moving seems never to have crossed her mind. That's partly because as much as Gowanus Houses has over the decades become a red-brick mini-city in the heart of rapidly gentrifying Boerum Hill, in Ms. Flowers's eyes much of the original spirit endures. "This is a place filled with great people who work hard every day to raise a family and put their kids through college," she says. "And the families still stick together. One thing about Gowanus Houses: there's no problem going up to the parents and telling them if a kid seems to be in trouble. In that way, it's like the old days. It really does take a village."

# 29

# A Moment of Remarkable Optimism

## Nick and Sally Webster on the Upper West Side

JUNE 20, 2010

Nick and Sally Webster, pioneer settlers in the West Side Urban Renewal Area, in their twice-renovated brownstone. (Suzanne DeChillo/*The New York Times*)

ALF a century on, it's hard to remember the starry-eyed idealism that marked the birth of the West Side Urban Renewal Area, the widely praised effort to replace 20 blocks of festering slums with housing for a broad mix of social and economic groups. But Albert and Sara Webster remember.

The Websters—Nick and Sally to everyone who knows them—are 72. But in the early '60s, when the urban renewal plans were being hatched, the couple were recently married 20-somethings from suburban New Jersey drawn together partly by a shared desire to live in New York. In 1963, they and another couple began the paperwork required to buy adjoining brownstones on 94th Street near Columbus Avenue.

The Websters' building, for which they paid $25,000, dated back to the 1890s and had once been a handsome dwelling. By the time the structure came to the couple's attention, it was dilapidated and had spent decades as a rooming house, with some of its dozen apartments lacking even a window. Rats and drug paraphernalia were the block's defining elements; gunfire followed by the whine of police sirens was its sound track. It would take five years, interminable paperwork, and a $90,000 gut renovation before the Websters could move in.

Despite the neighborhood's troubles, those were heady times, punctuated by protests against the Vietnam War, the burgeoning civil rights movement, and stirring sermons on behalf of both causes at nearby Riverside Church. The world around the Websters was being remade even as they were seeking to remake their corner of the world.

The goal in the urban renewal area—to create an economically integrated neighborhood that included housing for the poor, the middle class, and those who could afford a degree of luxury—was one the Websters embraced. "We were tuned into the whole ethos," Mr. Webster says. "All the things that people were talking about, those were the things we believed in." His wife felt the same way. "It was a moment of remarkable optimism," she says. "This was going to be an integrated neighborhood, with housing for people at every income level. What could be a more inspiring prospect?"

Not everyone shared their lofty sentiments. "My mother, who by then lived on Sutton Place, had a heart attack when she learned what we were doing," Ms. Webster recalls. "She said to me, 'What will I tell my friends?'" Nor did anyone make the process of acquiring even a decrepit

161

building quick or easy. To underscore the point, Mr. Webster tells a story: "I remember spending one solid hour signing papers for a $160,000 construction loan. When I was done, the lawyer showed me two legal-sized drawers full of documents. 'That's for your loan,' he told me. Then he showed me a folder maybe an inch or two thick. 'That,' he said, 'was for the sale of the Empire State Building.'"

As the Websters struggled with paperwork, government regulations, bureaucracies, and the challenges of taking part in an ambitious social experiment, the world around them seemed to mirror the sense of upheaval. This is illustrated by an aging piece of paper that Mr. Webster unearths from his voluminous files. The document, which lists key dates in the acquisition and renovation of their brownstone, traces a timetable that begins in November 1963, the month President Kennedy was assassinated, with the notation "Investigation begun, lawyer engaged" and concludes in June 1969, the month of the Stonewall riots in Greenwich Village, with the notation "Final closing, FHA, Bowery." Every date in the history of their building reverberates with an event in the outside world.

The couple moved into the house in 1968. "We were still optimistic," Mr. Webster says. "But that's not to say that our life was easy or peaceful." By the 1970s, many of the high hopes fueling the renewal project had curdled as neighborhoods throughout the city teetered. "It was the time of 'Ford to City, Drop Dead,'" Mr. Webster recalls, citing the *Daily News* headline that summed up the federal government's response to New York's woes. "There were crack vials on our stoop half the mornings of the week. There were real challenges on this block."

Through it all, the Websters soldiered on. And in making and remaking their brownstone, they fell in love with two teams of architects—first Harold and Judith Edelman (Mr. Edelman was responsible for such memorable projects as the reconstruction of St. Mark's in the Bowery), then John and Connie Torborg. In tracing the history of their house, the couple mention the architects so often and with such affection, they could be members of the family. "We started out with Harold and Judy," Mr. Webster says. "I remember Harold and I did the initial planning over a dinner during which we consumed a fair amount of bourbon."

The first renovation transformed the brownstone into a relaxed and commodious home for the Websters and their two young children, with rental apartments on the top floors. The second renovation, which took place a decade ago, was carried out by the Torborgs and imparted a different aesthetic. "Harold was a full-blown Modernist, in the best sense of the word," Mr. Webster says. "His space conformed to how we would like to live in our own home." By contrast, his wife says, "The Torborgs gave us molding. That was a big difference. Harold would be rolling over in his grave to see the crown molding."

The latest renovation retrofitted a family house into a comfortably empty nest, one well suited to this stage in the couple's lives. Mr. Webster retired in 1990 as the executive vice president and managing director of the New York Philharmonic, and Ms. Webster retired this year as a professor of art history in the City University system. But both still lead busy professional lives. Mr. Webster sits on multiple boards of directors, and his wife is completing her fourth book, on the 1777 memorial at St Paul's Chapel in Lower Manhattan to General Richard Montgomery, the first officer to die in the Revolutionary War. As redefined, their house is accommodating these new roles.

"With the kids gone, our life took on a new dimension," Mr. Webster says. "Our first life was full of family. The second has more to do with our professional sides and with New York. We stepped into a life that was waiting for us and re-created the setting to match that life." As part of this transformation, their daughter's bedroom was remade into a sitting room and their son's bedroom converted into an office for Ms. Webster, with bookshelves that reach to the 12-foot-high ceilings and a towering library ladder.

One part of the house that has remained largely unchanged is the back garden, which is two houses wide and shared with the Websters' neighbors, Joseph and Donna Rosalie. A Japanese maple, planted as a sapling in 1980 by Mr. Webster and his son, now stands eight feet tall. In nice weather, the couple eat here, sometimes joined by their neighbors or the Torborgs, who live two houses down. Especially after the attacks of September 11, the garden, like many green spaces in New York, felt like a place of refuge.

Through two teams of architects, the house has retained its intimate feel, thanks to original brick walls, multiple working fireplaces, and cushiony window seats. A stack of wood sits next to the fireplace in the living room; in winter, the Websters pull up a table and watch the fire as they eat dinner. And over the decades, certain themes have continued to define the mood of the house.

One is Maine. Mr. Webster's roots in the state go deep; in the coastal town of Surry, his grandparents built a lakeside home, which he and his three sisters now own, and the couple spend part of the summer there. Before the state was discovered as a happy hunting ground for antiquers, the Websters were trolling its out-of-the-way corners. Their forays yielded, among various finds, a quartet of colorful oils of his parents' house, a painting on wood of a cormorant by a Maine artist named Phil Barter, and a folk-art assemblage by Tonee Harbert, another Maine artist, honoring a local hermit named Elmer.

In homage to one of Ms. Webster's many areas of interest, a wall is lined with works of art made by women, including a doll-sized white dress, hand-smocked and hand-embroidered by her grandmother, that was Ms. Webster's when she was a baby. Her husband's study stands as a shrine to a half-century career that began with his proud management of the Harvard Glee Club. Among the photos of classical music stars is one of the conductor Seiji Ozawa playing softball with Mr. Webster in Japan; as Mr. Webster remembers the occasion, he graciously allowed the game between Mr. Ozawa's team and his team (the New York Philharmonic Penguins) to end in a tie.

In the decades since the Websters bought and transformed their brownstone, the story of urban renewal has been written, rewritten, and rewritten yet again. On the West Side, the story was originally told from the point of view of idealistic families like the Websters, who hoped to ensure an economically mixed population while preserving some of the beautiful old buildings. Later analysts focused on the plight of the families forced out by redevelopment, even in places like the West Side, where urban renewal was handled with more finesse than elsewhere. The Columbia University psychiatrist Mindy Fullilove uses the term "root shock" to describe the impact of displacement, and even to this day, who knows what became of the vast majority of the area's original residents? The men, women, and children who once lived on these blocks, so few of whom remained—where did they end up?

Come the turn of the 21st century, the story of urban renewal would be retold yet again, offering a kinder assessment of master builder Robert Moses, the moving force behind nearly all of the city's redevelopment efforts. Perhaps the megaprojects he spawned weren't so bad, revisionist critics argue. Perhaps we could use a Moses today.

Despite the endless rewriting of history, the economically integrated neighborhood that excited the Websters half a century ago has long since become a reality. "In the middle of our block there's public housing," Ms. Webster says. "On one corner there's subsidized housing for the elderly. On the other corner there's middle-income Mitchell-Lama housing." Sprinkled among the larger buildings are impeccably restored brownstones like their own. "And," Ms. Webster adds, with a tip of the hat to the popular grocery around the corner on Columbus Avenue, "we all shop at Mani's."

# 30

# Elastic Elegance

## Alison West in Kips Bay

JULY 11, 2010

Alison West, a yoga teacher and stepdaughter of the writer Mary McCarthy, in her Kips Bay studio. (Jennifer S. Altman for *The New York Times*)

THE rambling apartment on the Left Bank of Paris where the writer Mary McCarthy settled in the 1960s was by all accounts an alluring place. The apartment is remembered not only for the dinner parties at which celebrated artists and literary figures gathered to savor Ms. McCarthy's cooking and drink copious quantities of wine but also for the décor. Even today, long-ago visitors wax rhapsodic about the William Morris wallpaper, the Meissen demitasse cups. They recall a front balcony edged with an ironwork railing that overlooked the Rue de Rennes and back windows that faced a convent garden. In Diane Johnson's novel *Le Divorce*, an apartment that's a dead ringer for Ms. McCarthy's enjoys a star turn.

It would be a stretch to compare these fabled digs to the home of Alison West, Ms. McCarthy's 56-year-old stepdaughter. Ms. West lives in a 378-square-foot studio in Kips Bay, a three-flight walk-up that has been hers since her graduate-student days in the mid-1970s. (Asked its exact dimensions, she pulls out a tape measure, just to be accurate.) But despite obvious differences in scale and lavishness, the shadow of her famous parent hangs over this apartment. Ms. West inherited or otherwise acquired great quantities of Ms. McCarthy's artworks, furnishings, and memorabilia. She also has hundreds of her books, many autographed by luminaries of the day. Every corner holds a reminder of one of the bright lights of 20th-century American letters.

Would that the most compelling reminder, the stuffed owl atop a bookcase, its white feathers graying with age, were also a relic from that Parisian apartment. That's not the case. The owl migrated here not from Paris but from the house in Castine, Maine, where Ms. McCarthy also lived. "I always thought my father got the owl from Deyrolle, the famous taxidermy shop on the Left Bank," Ms. West says in a lightly accented voice that reflects a childhood spent largely abroad. Or perhaps it was a gift from the poet Robert Lowell, a dear friend of Ms. McCarthy's and a longtime Maine neighbor. "In any case," she continues, "it was definitely in Mary's study. She loved all birds of prey, and she especially loved owls because they were the symbol of Athena, the goddess of wisdom."

Ms. West was 7 when her father, a foreign-service officer named James West, married Ms. McCarthy. Ms. West, who was one of three children from his previous marriage, wasn't always close to her stepmother, and

not surprisingly: Ms. McCarthy was hardly known for being the moth-
erly sort. But upon her death in 1989, Ms. West came to own much of
what gave the apartment in Paris such flair. By that point, Ms. West had
long been ensconced in her studio on East 29th Street, where she has
lived since she arrived in 1974 with a friend from New York University.
The friend married and moved away; Ms. West stayed. The original rent
was $140, even then a bargain. Today, at $700, it feels like a steal.

In those early years, Ms. West worked as an art historian, specializing
in 18th- and 19th-century French sculpture. There followed a career as
a choreographer; Anna Kisselgoff, chief dance critic of *The New York
Times*, praised one of her works as "startling and rich." Today she's a
well-known practitioner of yoga, serving as a teacher of yoga instructors
and as director of the Yoga Union Center for Backcare and Scoliosis,
around the corner from her apartment. Though as fragile looking as one
of the sweet peas that sit in a bouquet on an end table, she can stand on
her head for 45 minutes.

Every morning she gets up at 6 to meditate. Yet even without the presence of a slender blond woman sitting cross-legged on a cushion in a
corner, this space would exude tranquility. Strands of meditation beads
are draped over a tiny bronze ladder—a scala coelestis, or stairway to
heaven, as Ms. West calls it. Beneath a crystal dome, a diminutive skeleton has assumed the lotus position.

The sense of serenity is enhanced by the quality of the light. In the
morning, shafts of sun enter through the windows and are reflected by
the large mirror on one wall. The windows face curtains of ivy, and the
ivy, too, is reflected in the mirror. The mood extends even to the bathroom, where murals evoke a Tuscan landscape, the sky stained pale pink
to suggest the approach of evening.

The activities that Ms. West pursues within these walls are similarly
contemplative. Often she listens to Mozart, choosing from one of 170
CDs that contain the composer's complete works and are shelved on a library stepladder. When she wants to watch a movie, she hangs a 72-inch-
wide window shade that she bought at Home Depot onto hooks attached
to one of the bookcases and uses a Dell projector to create her own little
theater.

The first movie for which she used this contraption was *Laura*, Otto
Preminger's film noir starring Gene Tierney. "I sat here alone with a glass
of Champagne," Ms. West remembers. "And it was so remarkable, being
able to totally focus on the black-and-white images and their wonder-

ful texture, with the light coming from behind." In her opinion, no flat-screen, high-def alternative could come close to letting her duplicate this solitary, riveting experience.

Ms. West likens her apartment to a set of Chinese boxes because of the ease with which spaces assume multiple personalities. A narrow custom-made sofa upholstered with moss-green velvet doubles as her bed. ("With company, it's either a tight squeeze or very *intime*," she says with a trace of a smile.) A mahogany table opens to seat eight for dinner. Her kitchen, equipped with both desk and copper pots, doubles as an office, with pens and stamps stored in a wooden sewing chest that belonged to her aunt Hope. Pinned to a wall is a note from her longtime nanny that begins, "Ma chère et jolie princesse." The nanny, whose name was Maria and who was a cherished part of Ms. West's sometimes unhappy childhood, died four years ago, in a car accident in Paris.

The ingenious use of space continues into the hall, where party dresses hang on wooden pegs. A visitor leaving or entering can't help but brush past a black Nicole Miller number whose taffeta skirt rustles slightly over a bouffant petticoat.

But most remarkable is the extent to which the apartment showcases the life of a woman who died more than two decades ago. While Ms. West traces her overall aesthetic sense to her mother, Margaret Szmurak, Ms. McCarthy seems the greater presence. The pair of small bronzes shaped like the Great Sphinx sat on her desk. The chairs with arms carved in the shape of griffons were in her living room, as was a painting by a Russian artist named Leonid Berman depicting a high jumper in four different positions. The 18th-century marble-topped chest in Ms. West's hallway stood in Ms. McCarthy's dining room, and the writer herself comes alive in a photograph by Cecil Beaton and in the Larry Rivers portrait that graced the inside cover of her first novel, *The Company She Keeps*.

Perhaps most evocative of Ms. McCarthy and her milieu are the hundreds of books, many of them inscribed to her and her husband by the great writers of the day. "Dearest Mary and Jim," her close friend Italo Calvino wrote on the flyleaf of his novella *The Silent Mr. Palomar*. "To Mary from Edmund" is the inscription inside *Le Nouveau Savoir-Vivre*, a whimsical French how-to book about marriage and domestic life that was a gift from Edmund Wilson, a former husband. There are books signed by her friends Hannah Arendt and Shirley Hazzard, along with copies of the Red and Blue Guides that guided Ms. McCarthy and her husband on their travels half a century ago. To this impressive library Ms. West has added gems of her own, among them a first edition of

Solzhenitsyn's *The Gulag Archipelago* that had been smuggled out of the Soviet Union.

The reminders of Ms. McCarthy's life and times are fascinating. Yet if any single item captures the spirit of this quiet and unassuming space, it's the large print above the sofa by Ilya Kabakov, a Russian-American conceptual artist. Kabakov depicts a writer seated at a desk wearing an immense pair of blue angel wings, and in the image of the angel, Ms. West sees the story of her own life. "It's all about what yoga is, about how to be a kinder human being and how to respond to our better angels," she says. "And look at the writer. Look at the bed behind her. She seems to live in one room, just like I do."

# 31

# Elephants for Luck

## Bharati Kemraj and Her Family in Soundview, the Bronx

AUGUST 15, 2010

Bharati Kemraj and her mother in the house next to her father's Hindu temple in Soundview in the Bronx. (Chester Higgins Jr./*The New York Times*)

BHARATI SUKUL KEMRAJ, a 27-year-old reporter and producer for the Bronx's public-access television channel, lives with her parents and three of her five siblings in a brick and stucco house near Sound View Park in the Bronx. Her two older sisters, who have their own families, live nearby. And especially with five grandchildren coming and going, the premises bustle with noisy meals and youngsters underfoot. But even when Ms. Kemraj is here by herself, she's hardly alone. She's surrounded by dozens of Hindu gods and goddesses, tabletop deities who are made of plastic, porcelain, copper, and even marble, outfitted to the nines in jewel-tone outfits of silk and organdy, and draped with strands of beads and garlands of fresh flowers. The assemblage constitutes a virtual second family.

From the outside of this unassuming two-story house set back from a quiet Bronx street, you'd never imagine that the interior would house such a profusion of images from a distant culture. While we're reminded again and again that New York is a city of immigrants, that within a single school district in Queens more than 70 languages are spoken, it's sometimes still a shock to see firsthand how energetically these cultures thrive behind seemingly anonymous front doors.

Shiva, Krishna, Ganesh, and the rest are in attendance partly because faith plays so critical a role in the family's life. Ms. Kemraj's father, Pandit Vishnu Sukul Kemraj, is a Hindu priest, and her two brothers, 12 and 22, are following in their father's footsteps. But it's largely thanks to Ms. Kemraj's mother, Chandra Sukul Kemraj, that the family's living room feels like a lavishly appointed place of worship, or as Ms. Kemraj sums up the situation with both affection and understatement, "My mother lives in her own dreamy little world. And what you see in this house is the result."

The parents emigrated from Guyana in 1986, and Ms. Kemraj, the third child, arrived in New York a few years later, when she was 7. In 1994 the family bought a house near Pelham Parkway, and two years later Pandit Sukul Kemraj became the priest of Vishnu Mandir, a Hindu temple created from a single-family house that he bought on Noble Avenue near Westchester Avenue.

But his days were spent driving a school bus to support his family, and the additional hours he spent commuting between house and temple for twice-daily services proved onerous. So a few years ago he built a house for his family on the empty lot that he owned next to the temple; Ms. Kemraj used to watch as heavy machinery transformed the small grassy expanse. The house, which cost $350,000 to build, was completed in the fall of 2007, and the family moved in just in time for Christmas, which they celebrate even though they are Hindus. As if to underscore how pleased everyone is to be here, half a dozen welcome mats march up the path to the front door.

The house is attached to the temple, and Ms. Kemraj and her family are in and out so often that this place of worship feels like a second home. The main service, on Sunday morning, is an exuberant affair in which several hundred worshippers, the men in kurtas, the women in shalwars and saris, sit on the floor and pack the aisles, singing, reciting prayers, and sharing sweets. Exquisitely dressed statues of gods and goddesses, much like the ones in the Kemraj living room, line the walls. Music from drums, tambourines, harmonium, and brass bells fills the air.

Images from these services are included in weekly television programs devoted to the Hindu community that Ms. Kemraj produces for Bronxnet, the channel for which she works. But the family's house seems an equally holy place, and nowhere more than the altarlike assemblage of religious figures in the front window to whom the family pray every morning.

Ms. Kemraj reels off their names as if reciting a list of her friends: "Here's Ganesh, the god of knowledge, who has the head of an elephant and a trunk. Here's Shiva the destroyer, with the green snakes around his neck. Here's Rama, the demon slayer, with a bow and a quiver of arrows. Here's Ganga, the goddess of the Ganges, the holy river, sitting on the body of an alligator. Here's Krishna, with his flute, and here's Kali, with all the arms and the necklace of skulls around her neck to destroy evil."

The female deities wear vibrantly colored saris shot with gold thread and flecked with pearls, turquoise sequins, and rhinestones. Sometimes the figures are scented with incense. The entire history of Hinduism seems to be on display in this modest home, and the power of these inanimate figures is considerable. Despite their exotic trappings, these gods and goddesses express all-too-human emotions and behavior—wrath, jealousy, passion, revenge. Even to a nonbeliever, these creatures have an undeniable aura, and they certainly have compelling backstories.

If gods and goddesses keep watch over this household, elephants bring good fortune. "When we first moved to our new house," Ms. Kemraj recalls, "I remember giving my mom $100, and she used that, along with some of her own money, to buy a porcelain baby elephant." That elephant, which was made in India, stands on plump white feet and is adorned with painted flowers and gold tusks. "You can see that its trunk is up, which means good luck," Ms. Kemraj says as she strokes the animal's glossy back. Over the years, the baby elephant has been joined by others, each more adorable than the last. Some are hand-painted, splashed with gold, sprayed with glitter, and topped by rose-covered vases. Elephants that didn't seem sufficiently embellished when they arrived were further dolled up by Ms. Kemraj's mother, obviously a dab hand when it comes to wielding a paint brush.

Mrs. Sukul Kemraj has also worked her decorative magic on more unlikely subjects, among them porcelain dolls that have the look of Victorian milkmaids, complete with blond ringlets, fans, and lace party dresses. Thanks to her handiwork, one such creature sports a bindi, the red dot traditionally applied to the forehead of Southeast Asian women. Other dolls have been touched up with crimson lipstick, matching nail polish, and spider webs of henna on the backs of their hands. Still others resemble Barbies retrofitted for life halfway across the world. "Whatever she collects," Ms. Kemraj says, "she adds her own little touch of creativeness."

Her mother has also addressed the issue of pets in distinctive fashion. With so many grandchildren underfoot, having a dog seemed one chore too many. So Mrs. Sukul Kemraj installed a kennel's worth of china puppies near the front door, by the plastic-covered brown brocade sofas and the coffee table topped with a sequined pink and brown cloth.

With four children still living under the parental roof, space in the three upstairs bedrooms is tight. In the boys' room, a harmonium vies with a PlayStation. In Ms. Kemraj's room, tools of her trade like cameras threaten to crowd out her collection of silvery Indian bangles.

The parents' room accommodates a set of bunk beds where the grandchildren sleep when they're visiting, and Ms. Kemraj sometimes sleeps there, too. She realizes that 27 is a little old for this sort of thing, but especially these days she feels fortunate to be safely ensconced in the parental nest. "With the economy in the shape it's in," she says, "I feel lucky that I can live here with my family." And something else keeps her rooted here, at least for now. "Back in Guyana, people always think about coming to America and making a better life for themselves," she says. "Here in New York, we don't make so much money. We can't spend and spend. But having stuff around that you like means a lot."

# 32

## A Young Life

### Elizabeth Weatherford and Murray Reich in SoHo

SEPTEMBER 26, 2010

Elizabeth Weatherford, an anthropologist, and her painter husband, Murray Reich, in their SoHo loft. (Benjamin Norman for *The New York Times*)

I N front of a SoHo boutique called Sabon, a young woman with a
punk haircut hawks freshly cut soap. In a shop around the corner,
sequin-trimmed dresses wink in the window. Tourists lugging oversized
shopping bags and chattering in every language known to man mob
the streets. But in a quiet fourth-floor loft on Spring Street near Greene
Street, in a cast-iron building where until 40 years ago workers cut fabric
for hospital scrubs, a fragment of old SoHo is preserved as if in amber.

The loft's residents are Murray Reich, a 78-year-old painter and longtime Bard College professor who studied with the abstract expressionist
Robert Motherwell, and his wife, Elizabeth Weatherford, the 65-year-old
founding director of the Film and Video Center of the Smithsonian Na-
tional Museum of the American Indian in Lower Manhattan. The couple
have lived in the loft for nearly four decades and witnessed the creation
of the neighborhood in its modern-day incarnation.

Mr. Reich, who was born in the Bronx, and Ms. Weatherford, who
grew up in Memphis, met in time-honored fashion in Paris in the summer of 1967. She was backpacking around Europe not long after graduation from college, and they crossed paths in the studio of Constantin
Brancusi, where Mr. Reich inquired of the pretty young blonde admiring
the sculpture, "Mademoiselle, are you French?" The two spent a little
time together, and he was immediately smitten; but before they could
exchange phone numbers, Ms. Weatherford had sped off on a motorcycle
to Rome.

"And so when I got back to New York, I went into a phone booth
with a handful of quarters and called every Weatherford in Memphis,"
Mr. Reich remembers. "I remember all those Southern accents. They'd
say things like, 'We had an Elizabeth, but she died.'" Then one day he
got a phone call. The mystery woman from Paris had turned up in New
York, and in short order the two were sharing an abandoned industrial
space in Chinatown.

That was in the late 1960s, a time artists were colonizing the empty
cast-iron buildings south of Houston Street. In 1972, just after Mr. Reich
won a Guggenheim fellowship, an artist friend approached him with a
proposition. Would he like to join three artists who were buying an old
garment factory and converting its lofts to residential space? For a total cost of $146,000, each family would have an entire floor containing
3,200 square feet of space. "So we put down $10,000 and got a mort-

gage of $26,500," Mr. Reich recalls. "Sounds inexpensive, right? But remember, these were 1972 dollars."

People familiar only with a SoHo defined by Prada and hordes of shoppers can't imagine how desolate the neighborhood was in those years, and how spartan the living conditions. At the turn of the previous century, the district south of Houston Street was home to much of the city's light industry, its tool and die factories and its silk-screening plants. By the late 1950s, those businesses had largely disappeared, soon to be replaced by artists like Chuck Close, Frank Stella, and Richard Serra, who set up shop in the buildings the manufacturers had left behind. "The city was being transformed economically right beneath our eyes," Ms. Weatherford recalls. "We were literally watching the first steps that manufacturing took as it moved out of New York and eventually as far away as China."

Other changes were afoot. Galleries such as Paula Cooper, OK Harris, and Max Hutchinson, where Mr. Reich had two exhibitions, established beachheads near Fanelli's Café, a fixture of the area seemingly forever. But even with the gradual influx of artists, the neighborhood was sparsely settled and, especially on weekends, virtually deserted. At night, footsteps echoed on empty cobblestone streets. City officials sometimes discovered that people lived in a building only when a fire broke out. "It was unbelievably hard," Mr. Reich remembers. "You couldn't buy a quart of milk. If you were visiting someone, they'd throw the keys out the window."

Such inconveniences were the least of it. Even today, Mr. Reich struggles to describe the chaos that greeted the couple when they took possession of their loft. Rats scurried about as if they owned the place. Decades' worth of lint was embedded in the wood floor. The rackety boiler reminded Mr. Reich of a 19th-century steam engine. Heat, hot water, and electricity were sometime things.

Relations among the building's owners, a group that shifted over the years, compounded the problems. Mr. Reich got on famously with the artist Stephen Posen and his wife, Susan, whose son Zac would grow up to be one of America's most lionized fashion designers. But a few relationships were less harmonious, especially early on, and this proved an issue when it came to the freight elevator, which was originally hand-operated. "If you were downstairs and the elevator was upstairs," Mr. Reich recalls, "you needed someone to bring it down for you. And if you and the person on the top floor weren't speaking, you had a problem."

Sleeping on a mattress on the floor and living in bare-bones fashion, the couple gradually reclaimed the space. As an artist, Mr. Reich knew how to work with tools, and together they covered the original floor with lengths of pine and refinished the floor-to-ceiling columns—actually trunks of pine trees—that run along the spine of the loft. With the help of young artist friends, they patched the holes in the ancient tin ceiling and constructed the living space.

"We had no money," says Mr. Reich, who along with his wife was teaching college part-time. "And we literally had to rebuild the place. Plumbers who came to help us would say, 'How can you live here?' But it was exciting. I think of that period as the good old days. It was a young life."

The loft also stands as mute testimony to an era in which artists could make lives for themselves without giving much thought as to whether such lives would make them rich. "Our lives were never simply about making money," Mr. Reich says. "That was never the primary concern."

When it came to furnishings, the neighborhood's rapidly changing face proved the couple's salvation. With local factories shutting down fast, castoffs were increasingly easy to find on the street, among them oak office chairs and desks outfitted with the original iron hardware. Forties-era cast-aluminum Magnalite cookware was acquired from a discount store on Canal Street and, for $400, a six-burner Garland stove from a place on the Bowery. From a salvage operation in Connecticut came a pink sink embedded in a slab of oak. Somewhere else the couple found cabinets with milk-glass tops and shallow drawers that had been used to store dental instruments and still smelled faintly of ether.

As with most lofts at the time, half the space served as a studio and the rest was residential, with the configuration of spaces shifting over the years to accommodate evolving needs. After the couple's son, Zeke, was born in 1981, his room was moved from spot to spot, and though Zeke is long gone from the premises, the army of Japanese robots that he played with as a child—outlandish-looking creatures of red, black, and silver metal that convert to guns and airplanes—remains perched on a shelf above the kitchen, ready to once again take on the world.

Both Mr. Reich and Ms. Weatherford are inveterate collectors of inexpensive things, and many pieces they own recall a forgotten moment in America's past—notably the two dozen hat forms carved from ash by Italian craftsmen, each for a different style of ladies' headgear. The sleek, sculptural-looking creations, which come apart like Chinese puzzles so the finished hats can be removed, are reminders of an era in which no woman ventured outside with a bare head.

The couple also have a remarkable collection of tramp art. Beneath the glass on the coffee table lies a tiny quilt made of strips of golden silk, bearing names like Quincey and Blackstone and Juniors, that were used to wrap cigars in the late 19th century. From semi-junk stores come intricate wooden fans, each carved from a single block of pine that has been sliced into paper-thin strips. The décor includes "crown of thorns" frames, a mirror framed by postage stamps made by nuns from Quebec, a house built of matchsticks, mirrors made of shells, a box constructed of Popsicle sticks. Everything, it seems, used to be something else.

And nearly everything seems to incorporate fragments of the past. Nineteenth-century "memory jugs" are plastered with odds and ends like buttons, bobbins, and a minuscule doll with a broken leg—"all the things they found in their cabinets," Ms. Weatherford says. A knife-art cigar box was crafted by a soldier from the 122nd New York Volunteers who lived in a home for Civil War veterans. Chains made from single pieces of wood were carved by Ms. Weatherford's great-grandfather during the Civil War when he was held in a Union prison at the mouth of the Delaware River.

Ms. Weatherford has long since left the South, but after her mother died a decade ago, many items that furnished her family home made their way north, among them a grandfather clock from the 1830s on which painted images of a setting sun and a rising moon move with the passing hours. Intermingled among the collection of little purses that hang on her bedroom wall is a fluffy number made of yellow ostrich feathers that belonged to a great-aunt, "a lively lady, a flapper," as Ms. Weatherford describes her. The loft is also home to Mr. Reich's paintings, which in recent years have featured images of arrows, a symbol he finds powerful and ambiguous.

You might think that a couple so deeply rooted in old SoHo would mourn its passing. Yet much as they savor the memory of the years in which they and their friends were the neighborhood's hardy pioneers, they have considerable affection for what SoHo has become. "It's a successful and dynamic part of the city," Ms. Weatherford says. "People leave each other alone. And they shop and enliven the neighborhood. There's something great about that." Her husband agrees. "The street life is so interesting," he says. "These days, everyone comes to SoHo."

# 33

## The Rebel Girl of Borough Park

Mary Sansone in Borough Park, Brooklyn

JANUARY 30, 2011

Mary Sansone, a 94-year-old resident of Borough Park, Brooklyn, where she has lived for more than half a century. (Chester Higgins Jr./*The New York Times*)

N 1956, the year Dwight Eisenhower was reelected to the presidency, Elvis Presley was burning up the airways, *My Fair Lady* was packing them in on Broadway, and Clairol was posing the eternal question, "Does she or doesn't she?" an Italian-American couple named Zachary and Mary Sansone bought a two-story brick house in Borough Park, Brooklyn.

Mr. Sansone worked on the docks, his wife was a social worker, and the couple had two small children. Since their marriage seven years earlier, they had lived mostly with Mrs. Sansone's mother in the amorphous area then known as South Brooklyn, in a house that Mrs. Sansone's grandmother had bought for $400 and that would fetch $3.5 million a century later when the neighborhood was anointed as Carroll Gardens.

The Sansones' single-family house, on 59th Street near New Utrecht Avenue, cost $14,000. "But once we made the $2,000 down payment," Mrs. Sansone recalls, "and with the $100 a month for the mortgage, we didn't have a nickel left over to furnish it." As it turned out, furnishings wouldn't prove a problem. Starting in her teens, Mrs. Sansone had been deeply involved with organizations that helped people in need. As a social worker with extensive connections in and out of government, along with a passion for righting social wrongs, she had a knack for untangling bureaucratic knots. Over the years, she had achieved an impressive track record in aiding people with problems, and thanks to the gratitude and generosity of those she assisted, some of whom had been waiting for years until she had a home of her home, the house on 59th Street became furnished as if by magic.

The crystal chandelier in the dining room? "I knew a couple of guys who wanted to get into the electricians' union," Mrs. Sansone says. "I'm a union person. They realized I needed a chandelier, and they bought me a chandelier."

The mahogany dining room set? "A man I knew had a son in the Army, and I helped him get out," Mrs. Sansone says. "I explained that he was the only child and that he had medical problem." Turned out the father was in the furniture business, and after Mrs. Sansone came to the aid of his son, the father said to her, "Mary, when you get married, choose the furniture you like and I'll get it for you." She ended up paying the discount price of just $500 for a dining table, six matching chairs, two buffet tables, and a breakfront.

The pink and white lusterware pitchers came from a man whose son was having problems in school and whom she helped get into a better school. The white china dinnerware came from a man in the housewares business whom Mrs. Sansone helped save from being deported back to Italy. The silverware service for 12 came from a young man whom she helped get into medical school in Bologna. "He offered me money," Mrs. Sansone says. "I told him no, I couldn't accept money, but he could wait for a holiday and give me something then." Today, eyebrows might be raised over such transactions, but back then attitudes were considerably more forgiving.

The recipient of these gifts, who is now 94, had come to her involvement with social causes early on. Her father was an organizer for the Industrial Workers of the World, and in 1924, when his daughter was 8, he took her to Union Square and plopped her atop a soapbox while he spoke to the crowds. By the age of 15, she was helping him organize workers in the garment district. Mrs. Sansone still has his small, worn copy of the *Little Red Songbook*, a collection of labor songs. "Rebel Girl," one of her favorites, would prove her lifelong anthem.

In 1964, Mrs. Sansone and her husband founded the Congress of Italian-Americans Organization, a social services group known by the acronym CIAO, whose early meetings were held in the couple's wood-paneled basement. In 1988, Mrs. Sansone founded a group called CURE (Community Understanding for Racial and Ethnic Equality). And those were just two chapters of a life devoted to the pursuit of social justice in a variety of arenas. "Gays, women, unions, human rights, civil rights," she says, "I'm there."

Over the decades, Mrs. Sansone has been close to nearly every politician who mattered in New York and many beyond the city's borders. A color photograph of President Obama leaning over to hug Mrs. Sansone at an event in Lower Manhattan is taped to the refrigerator, next to a picture of a beady-eyed Mary, age 6 months, wearing a white dress with puffy sleeves and, as someone once observed, "looking tough even then." The civil rights leader Bayard Rustin, a dear friend, ate spaghetti at her dinner table. Former mayor Giuliani, another close friend, feasted on roast veal and rigatoni with meatballs. Mayor Bloomberg gave her a key to the city. Robert Kennedy came to visit. Over the years, Mrs. Sansone's house became a political Lourdes for those who were eager to court the ethnic and working-class vote. "Politicians and community leaders were in and out day and night," she says. "The place was never empty."

And though at 4-foot-11 Mrs. Sansone is famously diminutive, she was no creampuff and never lacked for a comeback. A favorite story has to do with the 1977 mayoral race, when she was supporting Mario Cuomo, and Meade Esposito, the powerful Brooklyn Democratic boss, was backing Ed Koch. "Meade got hold of me one day and said, 'You forget I'm county leader,'" Mrs. Sansone recalled. "And I said, 'You forget I don't give a damn.'"

Along with the memories of endless political activity, the house on 59th Street is furnished with more than half a century's worth of domestic memories, notably photographs of the couple's daughter, Carmela, a psychologist who lives in New Jersey, and their son, Ralph, who was a judge. In 1986, at the age of 32, Ralph died in a small-plane accident, and the framed needlepoint images of flowers hanging above the buffet speak to his mother's anguish after his death, a loss that left her and her husband devastated for years.

"I couldn't sleep," Mrs. Sansone says. "I used to wake up in the middle of the night and write him letters. I did that every night. That's how I survived." The letters were passionate outcries that cursed God—not an easy sentiment for a lifelong Catholic to express—and she eventually threw them away. She also spent those hours doing needlepoint—anything for a brief distraction—and the fruits of those nights are visible on her walls.

Beyond the shattering personal loss, she feels there was a larger loss. Ralph Sansone had been the founder of the New Era Democrats, a political action group that supports candidates for public office without regard to their party affiliation. Had he lived, his mother believes that he would have been the child to carry on her political legacy.

These days the house feels especially empty. Mrs. Sansone's husband of 60 years—"my guiding star," as she calls him—died last June, at the age of 93. Hundreds of newspaper clippings, ceremonial programs, and other scraps of paper that trace the arc of the couple's life are bundled into a turquoise leather scrapbook that also contains encomiums from close friends like the writer Nicholas Pileggi, to whom Mrs. Sansone was a second mother. Mr. Pileggi once described her as an Italian Mary Worth and complained that there weren't enough words in the English language to do justice to her achievements.

Yet in many respects these rooms have changed very little since the Sansones arrived more than half a century ago. The floral-patterned drapes atop muslin curtains, the old-fashioned radiators, and the white lace tablecloth seem relics of another time. The red carpet, a new addition, arrived 25 years ago. The living room is still dominated by the couple's wedding picture, enclosed in a gold frame, in which Mrs. Sansone wears a dress with a train that looks like a giant fishtail. Above the fireplace hangs an enormous oil of a young Mrs. Sansone at her desk at CIAO, the Statue of Liberty raising her lamp proudly in the background.

Successive waves of ethnic change have transformed the world outside her front door, so much so that in this onetime Italian stronghold, she's the only Italian left on her side of the block. But CIAO's office is still around the corner, although after her husband's death she stopped making daily visits.

Now that Mrs. Sansone is alone in the house, a medical student named Jean-Luc Charlot, who's a friend of her grandson's, stays there to keep an eye on her. One of the few signs of Mrs. Sansone's age is the mechanically operated chair that carries her up and down the narrow staircase. The chair had been installed for her husband, but his widow is grateful for its presence.

The rooms upstairs also seem redolent of the past. Mrs. Sansone's bedroom is furnished with a mahogany four-poster bed and other pieces she inherited when her daughter was divorced, along with a canary named Ralph and a 100-year-old gold jewelry box. "It's antique," Mrs. Sansone says of the jewelry box. "But then I'm pretty antique myself."

# Palaces and Jewel Boxes

# 34

# For a Family, Elaborate Elbow Room

## Ted Brown and His Family on Staten Island

JUNE 28, 2009

Dr. Ted Brown and his family in their Victorian mansion on Staten Island. (Kate Glicksberg for *The New York Times*)

IN 1888, a German-born beer baron named George Bechtel who was said to be the wealthiest man on Staten Island gave his 21-year-old daughter Annie an extraordinary wedding present. Annie was betrothed to a German-American glass manufacturer named Leonard Weiderer, and the gift was a three-story, 24-room Victorian mansion in the Queen Anne style. The 4,500-square-foot showpiece, located on the charmingly named Mud Lane, contained eight bedrooms, two kitchens, and six fireplaces, each of a different design.

Annie's bridal home was adorned with every detail beloved by Victorian domestic architects—hipped roofs, gables, fish-scale shingles, chimneys, bay windows, dormer windows, even a turret. Garlanding the exterior were balconies and small terraces known as consumption porches that within a few short years would prove sadly appropriate. Inside, double oak doors led to a foyer dominated by a floor-to-ceiling mantel that was surrounded by imported tiles decorated with sunflowers, a popular motif of the day. Two dozen imported stained-glass windows, courtesy of Leonard Weiderer's glass business, exploded with stars, sunbursts, crescent moons, and floral designs pricked in luminous primary colors. Chestnut and oak paneling covered nearly every inch of wall space. As a student of Victoriana observed a century later, "The incredible Queen Anne was the home to beat" as far as 1890s Staten Island was concerned.

But the couple's time in the house was brief. Tuberculosis, a largely fatal disease in the late 19th century, claimed Mr. Weiderer's life just four years into the marriage; so much for all those consumption porches. His young widow moved to Germany and married a second time, but five years later, in 1899, she too died, of appendicitis. She was 31.

Annie's sister Agnes lived in the house until 1928, followed by the Teitelbaums (1928–48), the Fraziers (1948–88), and from 1988 to 1999, a French chef who slathered interior and exterior with what a paint consultant described as a "Lucille Ball shade" of pink. Mud Lane had long since been rechristened St. Paul's Avenue; the original name survived only thanks to the local historical society. Yet through all these incarnations, the house proved a survivor, the undisputed if neglected star among nearly a hundred handsome Victorians in the Stapleton section of the island. All it needed was someone who cared enough about its past to recapture its former glory.

That person turned out to be a soft-spoken Montana-born doctor named Ted Brown. Dr. Brown, the 63-year-old research director of the state Office of Mental Retardation and Developmental Disabilities, specializes in autism research and works out of offices on Staten Island. At the time he began house hunting in this neighborhood, he and his family were ensconced in a two-century-old farmhouse on Long Island, and he was developing a taste for residences with the trappings of history. When he was shown what a real estate agent described as an "older house of character," he was blown away. "Maybe I was crazy, but I just thought it would be fun to live there," Dr. Brown says in his understated way as he and his wife, Donna, sit side by side in what they call their formal parlor, an octagonal space framed by a sweeping archway.

Ms. Brown, a speech therapist who works with autistic schoolchildren (the couple met at a genetics conference in Australia), remembers the sequence of events differently. "When I first saw the house," she says, "I thought Ted had lost it."

When the couple bought the house in 1999 for about half a million dollars, they set aside $250,000 for renovations, a figure that ballooned to $400,000. Before moving in, they worked for six months on the interior; once in residence, they tackled the outside. Painting the façade, using sun-drenched colors like squash, copper, and antique gold, took five months. To choose appropriate colors, the Browns pored over books on Victorian architecture, traveled to Cape May, New Jersey, a capital of painted Victorians, and went through 20 quarts of paint, mixing and matching to achieve the 11 different shades they wanted.

"The first couple of years, the house was really in sad shape," Ms. Brown says. "We were really overwhelmed. Then we began to love it." But they know their work will never be finished, in part because the family, which includes the couple's 17-year-old son, Hunter, and their 19-year-old daughter, Montana, use all 24 rooms, incredible as that seems.

The room where the Browns are sitting this day has the look of a well-dressed stage set for some Victorian-era drama. An inlaid chessboard sits atop an inlaid table, and Debussy rests on the music stand of the grand piano. (Dr. Brown, who as a teenager was a state chess champion, plays both the game and the instrument.) The mantel is hidden beneath a flotilla of crystal baubles—bells, goblets, paperweights, teardrop candlesticks. A velvet shawl edged with ivory fringe hangs over a chair, and needlepoint pillows nestle in the corners of the sofa. Atop a Persian carpet from Dr. Brown's childhood home, one of two family dogs snuffles in his sleep.

From the front parlor, you can see the grand staircase, which resembles a puzzle composed of intricately braided chestnut spindles and a matching woven screen, each tiny curl milled separately. At the base of the stairs, a pair of linked circlets have been carved into the wood, an emblem, Ms. Brown thinks, of the union of the young couple whose time in the house was so brief and tragic.

The second floor is devoted to bedrooms, and a hallway on the third floor, the onetime servants' quarters, leads to the little two-story room at the top of the turret. On a Web site that lists the Brown house as a desirable location for filming and fashion shoots, the passageway to the turret is described as a "creepy, coffin-shaped tunnel," and creepy is the word. "When we first moved in," Dr. Brown says, "the kids used to play there, and someone was always being dragged in and locked away and had to be rescued." Far below unfold the expansive grounds that surround the house, punctuated by a 21-foot well and planted with poppies, peonies, and other staples of the Victorian garden.

New York is filled with beautiful old houses, but few receive the care that has been lavished on this one. The Browns know that they're helping to preserve a small but unique aspect of the island's history, and they're grateful to be doing so. "We feel as if we're taking care of her," Ms. Brown says of the house.

Dr. Brown especially couldn't be a more ardent steward. Upon moving to Stapleton, he joined the Mud Lane Society, the preservation group that helped get 92 Victorians designated as city landmarks, and as the group's president since 2007, he knows more than most people about what life in this part of the city was like a century ago. Though his professional life is focused on cutting-edge research, he cares deeply about the island's often overlooked past. Photographs that bring to life the brewers who were island royalty before Prohibition brought them low hang along the glorious staircase, and thanks to eBay, Dr. Brown has amassed a collection of old bottles from the Bechtel brewery.

He has also discovered that living in such an over-the-top house is just as much fun as he thought it would be. Strangers stop and take pictures, in part thanks to Forgotten New York, a Web site that proclaims 387 St. Paul's Avenue as "possibly the most gorgeous private dwelling on Staten Island and a contender for most beautiful building in NYC." And for the Browns, the history of the house only enhances its appeal. "This was a wedding gift for a bride," Ms. Brown points out. "Don't you wish you could give your child such a gift?"

# 35

# Enter, Hammering

## Sturgis Warner in the East Village

**NOVEMBER 8, 2009**

Sturgis Warner, a theatrical director, in his fifth-floor walk-up opposite the Public Theater in the East Village. (Robert Stolarik for *The New York Times*)

S TURGIS WARNER'S fifth-floor walk-up opposite the Public Theater in the East Village is filled with amazing things. A bookcase made from a door hangs from the rafters. A washing machine tucked under the bed rolls over to the kitchen and plugs into the sink. But few contraptions are more ingenious than the bathroom that converts—cue the applause!—into a fully equipped darkroom where Mr. Warner, a longtime actor and theater director, used to process the pictures he took of his own productions. Blackout curtains unfurl as if by magic, a wooden table with a sink for washing prints lowers onto the tub, and an enlarger swings down from the ceiling, thanks to an intricate system of pulleys operated by 120-pound barbells.

"It took a while to figure out," says Mr. Warner, a rangy 59-year-old with intense blue eyes, a shock of silvery hair, and a plummy voice that befits one in his profession. "But from set building, I learned to solve problems. I learned creative solutions to dealing with small spaces. It was a fun project. Actually, it was more fun to build than to do darkroom work. I think I'm a better carpenter than darkroom guy."

Mr. Warner's skills as a builder and designer of sets are indeed formidable, and those skills served him well when it came to confronting the challenges presented by his apartment, a high-ceilinged 700-square-foot space with a complicated history.

The apartment sits like a red-brick hat atop Colonnade Row, a series of marble town houses on Lafayette Street fronted originally with 27 matching Corinthian columns. When Colonnade Row was erected in 1833, there were nine houses, and an address on this part of Lafayette Street represented the height of fashion. By 1903, however, only four houses remained, and a strip once considered the city's most elegant was experiencing hard times.

As a child growing up in Washington, D.C., Mr. Warner would never have predicted that he would end up in the heart of the East Village arts scene. As a teenager, he was the ultimate jock—no surprise for a kid who eventually shot up to 6-foot-9. "I wasn't much of an intellectual in those days," he admits. But in college he discovered theater, and he came to New York in 1973, moving into this apartment five years later when Bruce Mailman, the East Village entrepreneur who owned the building, made him an irresistible offer. "He told me he had an apartment he wanted me to move into but said it needed massive work,"

Mr. Warner recalls. "He promised to give me cheap rent in return for renovation."

In coming to New York and finding cheap digs in the heart of the cultural action, Mr. Warner did something that was still relatively easy for creative artists to do back in the 1970s. Initially, the rent was just $250, remarkably low even then, for what Mr. Warner describes as "a wreck." By 1982, the rent had bumped up to $350, and there it stayed until 1999, when Mr. Warner himself, grateful for the arrangement, raised it to $500.

His motives were not entirely altruistic. Eight years earlier, a modest little production by three performance artists who called themselves Blue Man Group and flung around blue paint and shaving cream had moved into the Astor Place Theater, which was housed on the building's ground floor. (The production would quickly develop from scrawny upstart to multinational behemoth, "the most exciting thing to happen in the American theater," as *USA Today* summed up its success according to the poster on the façade of Mr. Warner's building.) The year Mr. Warner voluntarily raised his own rent, the building was poised to be sold to the show's producers, and he surmised that a slightly higher figure would make him look more attractive to a future landlord.

Over the past three decades, Mr. Warner has transformed a ramshackle space whose walls were home to armies of mice and roaches into a smartly designed setting that serves as both home and office. In 1998, he founded the Twilight Theater Company, a low-overhead organization dedicated to the creation of new plays. Today he's the company's co-artistic director, and the apartment, which friends find as snug and efficiently organized as a ship's cabin, is used for meetings and rehearsals.

The thick wooden beams in the ceiling stayed, as did the brick walls and the original windowpanes. But virtually everything else is different. Mr. Warner installed insulation between the beams where there had been only tar paper, roof board, and leaks. He built skylights, graceful arches, and a loft that functions as a guest room and storage area. A skilled electrician, he rewired the entire apartment. He sanded all the floors and built the bed, the couch, and other items of furniture using scraps of wood he found in Dumpsters. To make the place more commodious for his former wife (Mr. Warner was married for a time in the 1980s), he created a double-size clothes closet and a bathroom mirror framed with oversize bulbs—all very movie star. Because Mr. Warner designs and builds sets for his own shows, pieces of cardboard, great swaths of fabric, recycled wood, and random items of hardware are stashed in out-of-the-way nooks and crannies.

It would be no exaggeration to say that Mr. Warner is obsessively well organized; Actors Equity could pick up filing tips by riffling through his cabinets. His drawers are stuffed with *Playbills*, theatrical programs, and scripts dating back to the 1970s, meticulously organized by location (Broadway, Off Broadway), category (workshops, readings), and date.

As a reminder that a hard-core member of the city's theatrical community is in residence, red and white wooden signs that tout a play called *Comedians* and that Mr. Warner salvaged decades ago from the street are suspended from the ceiling. ("An Uproarious Romp"—A.P., "A Lot of Good Laughs"—NBC-TV, and "Majestically Funny"—*The Daily News*, in case you're wondering what the critics said when *Comedians* opened on Broadway in 1976.)

But Mr. Warner's days here may be numbered. The producers of Blue Man Group bought the building in 2001 and plan to use the apartments as their own residences, something that's allowed under the law. In preparation for this, they've already started taking steps to buy out tenants. In 2007, as a compromise measure, Mr. Warner signed a new two-year lease with Blue Man Group that raised his rent to $800; but that lease expired a few weeks ago, and his landlords have told him they won't renew it. Although he expects an eviction notice any day, Mr. Warner plans to take the matter to court and estimates that the fight could buy him at least a year. (As of mid-2012, he was still hanging on by his fingernails.) He's pinning his hopes on legislation pending in Albany that would protect him, and he's encouraged by a 2006 victory in the city's Housing Court that allowed him to keep his unusually low rent.

Mr. Warner is fighting to keep his apartment in part because he knows that replicating what he has, in terms of both space and quality, would be impossible. "We understand each other's point of view," he says of his landlords. "But to ask me to give this up is asking a lot. It's my blood, sweat, and tears."

He also sees his crusade as part of a larger and almost existential struggle. Year by year, young people find it increasingly difficult to come to New York and make careers for themselves in the arts, as Mr. Warner himself did decades ago. While complaints about the cost of housing in New York are the most familiar of litanies, for the person who comes to the city to try to make it as an actor or a painter or a musician, the lament is especially plaintive and the calculus involved increasingly challenging. That ever fewer people can live *la vie bohème* while keeping a roof over their head is something that young people who started out as Sturgis Warner did talk about all the time.

On a wall near a window that faces the Public Theater there hangs a tiny image of a handsome young man with shoulder-length hair. This is Mr. Warner's hack license, expiration date May 31, 1974, and a memento of his first job in the city. "When I first came to New York in 1973, I drove a cab twice a week, and it paid for everything," he says. "Today, kids need a full-time job just to make ends meet. There's no time to do young theater, to find your chops.

"To be an artist in New York, low overhead is everything," he adds. "It's what kept me in the city. If you have low overhead, you have a show."

# 36

# Pocket-Sized on West 47th Street

## Jonathan Cerullo in Hell's Kitchen

APRIL 25, 2010

Jonathan Cerullo, a choreographer, director, and actor, in his Hell's Kitchen studio. (Fred Conrad/*The New York Times*)

S OME of the multitudes who saw an early touring production of *Cats* in the mid-1980s might remember an exuberant orange tabby named Skimbleshanks. The character, aka the Railway Cat, was played by Jonathan Cerullo, a 20-something dancer who grinned out from behind hand-painted makeup, his body swathed from ears to tail in yak hair as he belted out Skimbleshanks's jaunty theme song.

In 1985, the year before stepping into Skimbleshanks's ratty-looking fur, Mr. Cerullo had moved into a 348-square-foot apartment in a century-old tenement on West 47th Street in Hell's Kitchen. The initial rent was about $300 a month, an exceptionally low figure even back then.

*Cats* has long since become a comic's punch line, and Mr. Cerullo has accrued an 11-page résumé of credits as a choreographer, actor, and director. But he has stayed put in this pocket-sized rent-stabilized space, for which he now pays just over $900.

In sinking such deep roots in this neighborhood, a longtime rough-and-tumble district defined by rowdy dockworkers as much as by proximity to the theater district, Mr. Cerullo was following in the footsteps of a generation of theater folk. Even in the early 20th century, the tiny apartments in the tenements lining these dreary blocks housed actors and their would-be brethren, who endured tight quarters in exchange for rakish ambience. Some of these troupers left behind reminders of their presence; a theatrical photographer who like Mr. Cerullo has lived for decades in the West 40s discovered a scrapbook bulging with memorabilia from a once celebrated, now forgotten turn-of-the-last-century actress.

Like many of his neighbors, Mr. Cerullo made a deal with the devil. In exchange for a still modest rent that has allowed him to follow his muse, he has compressed his domestic life into a minute space. Even for a struggling young performer who hadn't yet accumulated much in the way of possessions, the square footage was minuscule; some New Yorkers have roomier closets. The apartment can also be hot, dark, and confining. "The space is so small," Mr. Cerullo acknowledges, "it's easy to feel like you want to jump out of your skin."

Yet over the past quarter century, he has transformed his Lilliputian home in remarkable fashion. To visit his home is like stepping into a Fabergé egg; the little rooms are gaudy mélanges of intense colors (all those theatrical posters), shiny surfaces (a passion for Art Deco will do that), and castoffs reborn as retro chic. And like those phantasmagoric stage sets in which nothing is quite what it seems, every item collapses, converts to something other than what it appears to be, skates about on wheels, or opens to reveal an ingenious feat of design. "When guests come to visit, their jaws drop when they see what I've done with the place," says Mr. Cerullo, a still lithe 50-year-old with a personality as vivid as his décor. "They are floored by the transformative nature of it all. They are truly in awe."

When Mr. Cerullo first encountered the apartment, the space retained many of its original century-old features, among them tin ceilings, gas pipes for long-disappeared sconces, and pine floors edged with dark banding. The pocket shutters in the living room were encrusted with thick black paint, and a fireplace that once burned coal lurked behind a brick wall.

After considerable stripping, sanding, and refinishing—and the stiffened fingers to show for it—Mr. Cerullo set to work creating the special effects that give the apartment its now-you-see-it, now-you-don't quality. In the living room, a futon sofa on casters unfolds to become a double bed. A conference table stashed behind the sofa expands into a full-size dining table; on the eve of the new millennium, Mr. Cerullo served eight guests a seven-course dinner. The vintage coffee table perches on wheels, and a pair of red leather cubes provide storage for towels, sheets, and CDs. In the sliver of space between the living room and the kitchen that Mr. Cerullo calls his office, a computer table that swings down vertically from the wall saves precious inches. In the kitchen, so petite that if you stretch out your arms you can touch all four walls, artfully concealed plastic bins and wire baskets store everything from glassware to coat checks for Mr. Cerullo's jam-packed parties. And despite a full complement of electronic equipment, not a speck of wiring is visible. Cunningly designed strips of black plastic tubing that snake around the walls and ceiling conceal every strand.

What gives Mr. Cerullo's apartment its panache, however, isn't the cleverness of the details but the lavish—an unsympathetic observer might say over-the-top—decorative accents that reflect every aspect of his professional and personal life, along with a decided taste for the styles of the '20s and '30s.

From the ceilings hang a pair of Art Deco chandeliers—glittery concoctions of crystal, tin, and milk glass. They're joined by two mirror balls, a fixture of 1920s nightclubs long before the age of disco. "They revolved counterclockwise when the dancers moved clockwise, and they gave the dancers the sense that they were floating," Mr. Cerullo says.

"Whenever I need a little beauty, a little escape, I turn them on. It's not like I live in some la-la land. But when I'm entertaining, they create an entirely different ambience."

The baby kitchen is peopled with Hollywood's glamour girls and boys in the form of glossy black-and-white images by George Hurrell, photographer to bygone stars. Here are Hedy Lamarr, James Cagney, Joan Crawford, Mae West, Errol Flynn, and Clara Bow, as vivid as if just yesterday they were preening before the cameras. Mr. Cerullo tore the pictures out of a calendar and attached them to the refrigerator with magnetized metal clothespins.

Despite so many years in such tight quarters, Mr. Cerullo is an avid collector. He has amassed dozens of pieces of Chase chrome—electro-plated items in Art Deco design—that have been catalogued and that he hopes one day to give to the Wolfsonian, the design museum in Miami Beach. He has a trove of cardboard boxes, covered with decorative paper, that once held everything from pins and playing cards to soap and stationery.

Shimmer is provided by accents of crystal and silver that range from Art Deco martini shakers to the aluminum roofing tiles (500 for $12; thank you, Home Depot) that his science-teacher father, who assisted him with much of the construction, helped him glue onto the doors of the kitchen cabinets. Red paper flowers, along with matching votive candles and a tulip-shaped pressed-glass container filled with red marbles, provide blasts of color. The walls are also red, because in Mr. Cerullo's opinion, "red has a soul."

From the professional side of his life come dozens of theatrical posters for productions that run the gamut from *Anna Karenina* to the Big Apple Circus, along with items like a handwritten note from Samuel Beckett ("Thank you for your letter and kind birthday wishes," the playwright scribbled) and a signed poster with an image from Richard Avedon's series of photographs *Dovima with Elephants*. The signature is a trophy from the time Mr. Cerullo was working as an assistant director for an evening of Beckett on Theater Row. Knowing that Avedon was planning to attend a performance, Mr. Cerullo brought the picture to the theater for him to sign.

Bold-faced figures from the arts aren't the only individuals who populate this apartment. Mr. Cerullo comes from a sprawling Italian-American family with deep roots in New York, and sometimes every one of his relatives seems to be inhabiting these quarters in one form or another. Here's his mother, her hair in a little girl's black bob, standing beside an old-fashioned baby carriage in front of a house in the Bronx. Here's the red plastic radio she listened to when she was a teenager. Here are beaded hats made by Mr. Cerullo's grandmother, along with faded photographs of his great-great-aunt Erminia Frezzolini, a 19th-century soprano who was said to have inspired two operas by Verdi and in any case sang at their premieres at La Scala in Milan. "She also had a relationship with him," Mr. Cerullo says, framing the word *relationship* in air quotes. "At least there were always those little whispers in my family."

# 37

## Ardent Admirer, Devoted Steward

George Burke on Staten Island

DECEMBER 19, 2010

George Burke and his Staten Island mansion. (Hiroko Masuike for *The New York Times*)

WHEN George Burke was growing up on Staten Island in the 1930s and '40s, he used to ride horses with a pair of local sisters named Elizabeth and Belle Seguine. The Seguine girls, as they were called, lived in the island's Prince's Bay section in a Greek Revival mansion, a 16-room house that an ancestor named Joseph Seguine had built in 1838 on property Joseph's grandfather, James Seguine, had purchased half a century earlier. The colonnaded portico faced formal gardens, and a broad sloping lawn offered an expansive view of Raritan Bay. Seen for the first time, the house and its setting look like a mirage.

As befit the homes of wealthy families of the era—the Seguines had been big deals in the oyster-harvesting business, with a specialty in manufacturing pearl buttons—the interior dripped with paintings, antiques, and decorative plaster molding. George Burke, who even at a tender age had a taste for old houses, was smitten. "One day," he used to tell the girls' mother, Bess, "I'm going to own your house."

The Seguine sisters eventually married and moved away. Their mother moved away also, and the house, left empty, suffered from neglect. The original 200 acres were whittled down to 27 acres through development, and what land remained became so overgrown that the mansion itself was barely visible.

Mr. Burke, too, left the island, spending more than a decade in the Air Force, much of the time in Europe. While there, he visited the great museums of the Continent and shipped back 4,500 pounds of paintings and furniture. When he returned home, he ran a pair of restaurants and worked as an interior designer and as a color consultant for Sherwin-Williams, the paint company. A former president of the Staten Island Historical Society, he rescued several old houses on the island. Yet for reasons he himself might be hard-pressed to explain, the mansion by the bay remained an obsession.

In 1981, he got a phone call from Bess Seguine that would transform his life. "George, you've always wanted this house," said Mrs. Seguine, who was then in her 90s and close to death. "Now you can have it. But you must promise me that you will save it." She didn't have to ask twice.

Mr. Burke bought the house for $150,000 and spent the next five years restoring the premises, largely with his own hands. He so loves to recount the dramas involved—breaking his leg while fixing the roof, for example, and living for a year in a single unheated room—that he tells the stories again and again, practically word for word. And thanks to his efforts, the mansion looks much as it did when the Seguines roamed these generously proportioned, high-ceilinged rooms. It offers a portrait of how people lived in an era characterized by both graciousness and a crowd of servants.

The original owners are present in spirit, thanks to such inheritances as the Seguine family Bible, which sits open on a table in the center hallway, and a large oil of Joseph Seguine, a kindly looking man with soulful eyes. But the furnishings are almost entirely the 18th- and 19th-century antiques that Mr. Burke bought during his years abroad.

Persian carpets cover hardwood floors. Grandfather clocks stand at attention in corners. Crystal chandeliers dangle from decorative ceilings. China cabinets are stuffed with Dresden and Meissen. There are 10 working fireplaces—"Thank God," says Mr. Burke, who remembers heatless early days in the house. In the front parlor, where Mr. Burke can often be found with Rusty, his Doberman, curled up beside him on a sofa, French bisque shepherdess lamps perch atop end tables, and heavy pink and gray curtains—"bishop's sleeve drapes," Mr. Burke informs a visitor—frame the front windows. There's a reproduction of a candelabra that once graced the *Titanic*. In the rear parlor, sconces illuminate a black lacquer piano splashed with gilt. Decorative touches in the dining room include a huge silver meat dome—Sheffield, circa 1810—that housed Mr. Burke's Thanksgiving turkey. A mirrored cabinet holds crystal that belonged to Mr. Burke's mother and grandmother, the glittering reflections of pitchers and wine goblets extending as far as the eye can see.

In the place of honor of what Mr. Burke calls his hangout room, a rosewood-paneled space with a peacock fire screen, hangs a painting of his handsome mare, Lady Pizazz, a faded blue ribbon pinned to the frame. "She was a gorgeous horse," says Mr. Burke, whose eyes shine when he looks at the picture. "I miss her to this day."

The décor is dazzlingly eclectic—Victorian, French, Chippendale, Chinese Chippendale, you name it. Mr. Burke professes love for every item in the house, right down to the tiny star-shaped brass dust guards that keep dirt from collecting in the corners of the stair treads. But if pressed, he would probably say that his favorite possessions are the paintings, and not surprisingly, because so many of the big names are represented, among them Rubens, Joshua Reynolds, Thomas Gainsborough, and Rembrandt Peale.

This time of year, the house is lavishly decorated in preparation for Mr. Burke's annual Christmas party. Fir and tinsel garlands drape the walls and mantelpieces, and a huge tree hung with ornaments, many of them antiques, presides over the back parlor. Nor is Christmas the only occasion Mr. Burke plays host to a large gathering. His White Party in the spring is a major social event on the island, lavishly covered in the society columns of the *Staten Island Advance*, the local newspaper. At his Plantation Barbecue in the fall, men in high boots and feathered hats and women wearing hoop skirts and carrying fringed parasols feast on barbecued chicken, baked beans, and corn bread.

Despite the development that has eaten up so much of the island, Mr. Burke's property retains a bucolic feel. A stretch of Seguine Avenue, one of the streets bordering his spread, is still lined with Osage orange trees from China that were planted by Frederick Law Olmsted. The celebrated landscape architect lived for a time on the island and sometimes dined with the Seguine family on their terrace.

Thanks to the Seguine Equestrian Center, which sits on the southern portion of Mr. Burke's land, visitors can admire horses grazing in the distance. Set against a backdrop of stone fences, with a blue sliver of Raritan Bay visible in the distance, the horses give his property the look of a 19th-century landscape painting. Nor are they his only companions. Along with Rusty, his menagerie includes three chickens, a duck named Wilma, and a handful of peacocks who sleep in the trees and whose cries almost drown out the classical music that blares from loudspeakers. The size of the property, combined with the plethora of wildlife, makes Mr. Burke feel as if he has escaped, albeit momentarily, from the thrum of urban life. "Once I close my gates," he says, "I feel like I'm in my own little world."

The local paper describes Mr. Burke as an individual who "stands among Staten Island's pantheon of accomplished people, independent, a perfectionist, an antiques fancier, a solitary figure in his formal garden, a sort of heroic man struggling to preserve the past while battling against the encroachment of progress." Yet serendipity seems to have played a considerable role in bringing him to this setting. What if the mansion hadn't fallen into his hands? What if his military career hadn't sent him abroad, where he collected so many beautiful things? Would Mr. Burke, an odd mix of shy and sociable, still be helping Sherwin-Williams customers choose paint chips?

Yet here he is, at the age of 80, presiding over his domain like a lord of the manor or, as he puts it, like an old country squire. He also has one eye on the future. Although part of a large extended family, with many nieces and nephews, Mr. Burke never married and has no children. From early on he worried about what would become of the mansion when he wasn't around to care for it. And so in 1989 he transferred the house and its property to the Historic House Trust of New York City, which operates in conjunction with the city Parks Department. Under the terms of the arrangement, Mr. Burke can live in the house until his death, at which time the trust will take over the property. Because the building is a city landmark and is listed on the state and federal registers of historic places, Mr. Burke is confident that what he calls "the last of the island's great old plantation houses" will enjoy a long and happy life.

These days he couldn't be busier. Along with organizing his three annual bashes, for which food and drink are prepared in the two basement kitchens, he opens the house to the public four times a year. He recently created a tax-exempt organization to spearhead preservation of the house, with a fund-raiser planned for the fall. Friends constantly drop by, and as sole caretaker of the property, Mr. Burke has a never-ending list of tasks. Just last week he spent an entire day polishing the silver. One year he planted 3,000 bulbs. And did we mention his gold-leaf work?

Yet by all accounts, he wouldn't have it any other way. "The house makes him smile," says Mr. Burke's niece Linda Daller, who lives nearby and is as close to him as a daughter. "I think he never found a partner because the house was his partner. And besides, who else would take on such a responsibility?"

# Nesting

# 38

# Kitten Heaven

## Tammy Cross and Her Kittens on the Upper West Side

SEPTEMBER 13, 2009

Tammy Cross in the Upper West Side apartment that she shares with homeless kittens. (Tina Fineberg for *The New York Times*)

I F you love cats, kitten heaven is the old-fashioned bathroom in Tammy Cross's apartment in a Beaux-Arts building on the Upper West Side, where five balls of fluff, none bigger than a fist and some just two days old, are napping, reclining, or rolling about in various states of adorableness. "This is the nursery," explains Ms. Cross, who has been saving needy animals ever since she was a child growing up in Florida and Connecticut and retrieved baby squirrels that had fallen out of their nests. "This is where they stay when they're on the bottle."

As many of the city's cat fanciers know, Ms. Cross has for two decades been the guiding spirit behind Kitten Little Rescue. The organization does what its name implies—rescues sick, abused, or abandoned kittens—and shows them off on summer weekends at an Upper West Side street corner. The hope is that by being so enchanting, these creatures will attract adoptive families or at least foster parents willing to house them temporarily.

In many respects, the sunny one-bedroom apartment on Broadway near 86th Street, where Ms. Cross has lived for 15 years and for which she pays about $1,000 in rent, represents the group's mother ship. Here, some 6 to 18 baby kittens at a time, and once as many as 22, are bottle fed and nursed back to health. Over the years, perhaps 2,000 kittens in need have passed through her doors.

Ms. Cross, a vivacious, wisecracking 51-year-old, has lived a life defined by cats ever since she came to New York when she was 22. She gravitated to the city, she says, "because I didn't fit in anywhere else" and supported herself by working as a manager and booker at jazz clubs, all the while bouncing from one apartment to another.

The place where she lives now started out as a sublet. At the end of two years, the prime tenant signed the apartment over to her. "It's a real New York story," Ms. Cross says as she describes the convoluted but heartwarming chain of events that led to her good fortune. "You never know who your benefactors will be." Nor is this the only occasion that friends and sometimes even strangers have eased her way in the city; she can tell similar stories of out-of-the-blue kindness. It is as if Ms. Cross's New York is filled with guardian angels, poised to step from the shadows and lend a hand at every turn.

She, for her part, has created a welcoming, if modestly outfitted, refuge. And despite her near obsession with her small charges, you don't enter her apartment and immediately think, "Oh, my God, a crazy cat person lives here!" That is by design. "I live a pretty normal life," she says. "And at the end of the day, I've got to want to come home to my place."

At first glance, you see only a cheerful and, at 450 square feet, very cozy space. The carved oak fireplace in the living room is original to the apartment, as is the mirror that hangs above it. Sheer white curtains flutter at the windows. The living room walls were recently painted Jazz Age Coral by Ms. Cross's boyfriend, Ron McCormick, who paints restored houses along the Connecticut shore and thought the color appropriate in a building constructed shortly after the turn of the last century.

Mr. McCormick is part of her life thanks to the good offices of a close friend of Ms. Cross's. He had been her boyfriend when she was in her teens but had dropped off her radar until about 18 months ago, when the friend announced to Ms. Cross, "He was great. We've gotta find him." Ms. Cross was petrified by the prospect. "I was shaking in my shoes," she admits. "It had been 28 years since I'd seen him. I was 40 pounds heavier. The whole prospect was terrifying." Turns out she needn't have worried. Mr. McCormick is back in the picture, and he doesn't seem to be going anywhere soon.

Delighted as she is to have him around, initially she wasn't nuts about his contributions to her décor. "Ron, it looks like salmon," Ms. Cross complained when she saw his handiwork. He begged to differ. "It's true to the era," he insisted. To her dismay, he also painted the moldings white. "They're supposed to pop," Ms. Cross explains, sounding dubious.

As in other of the unrenovated apartments in this building, a former hotel, the kitchen is minuscule and has no stove. Nevertheless, using only a microwave, a convection oven, and a hot plate, Ms. Cross has whipped up Thanksgiving dinners for a dozen of her volunteers, who, along with contributions from the public, keep her rescue work afloat.

Still, make no mistake. Cats are in residence. Move the sofa, and a knot of cat toys appears. Don't watch where you're going, and you could accidentally step on a kitten, which is why Ms. Cross walks around the apartment barefoot. Mewing punctuates any conversation, as do phone calls from staff members at the city's animal shelter seeking to place strays that might otherwise almost certainly be euthanized. "Hey, Jess, how many?" Ms. Cross says into the phone this morning in response to one such call. "Single? How old? What color? Black and white? Of course. Send it over, honey. You got the address?"

And in every respect, this is a cat-friendly environment. Because kittens sometimes get extremely sick, the white slipcovers on the sofa and loveseat are washable, or as Ms. Cross says, "When it's so bad that the vet prescribes holy water, you have to be able to spray with Clorox." A swatch of gray industrial carpet wrapped around a door frame makes an ideal scratching post. There are three litter boxes, although they're emptied so religiously, you'd never know just by sniffing that this is what pet-supply manufacturers tactfully describe as a multiple-cat household. The only closet is packed to the rafters with cat carriers. In the bathroom, kittens that are Ms. Cross's specialty, those that are ill or very young or can't eat on their own, look up with piteous eyes.

Whether there will be quite so many cats in Ms. Cross's future is uncertain. She wasn't the only New Yorker to be shaken by the state of the city's economy after the attacks of September 11 and to wonder how she would be affected personally. "After 9/11, I spent a year or two being really scared—real heart-pounding anxiety," she says. "I felt like I was one month away from living in the park with 20 cats."

She thought she was too old to be a veterinarian—"plus I didn't think I was smart enough," she adds—but nursing seemed an option. "Also," she points out, "unlike a vet, who has to deal with everything—cows, horses, kittens—a nurse has to deal with just one species. I've been nursing critically ill kittens for 20 years. Really, it was a natural." She applied to nursing school, even though she had never gone to college and had lots of catching up to do. She dutifully completed the necessary prerequisites and in June received her degree from the Long Island College Hospital School of Nursing, along with an award for being the student "with the most particular love of nursing." Next step: passing the state boards and finding a job.

But she has no intention of forsaking the cause that is such an integral part of her life. This day she's sitting on the loveseat with Ducky—"because he follows me around like a duck"—nestled in her lap as she heats a tiny baby bottle filled with KMR—Kitten Milk Replacer—in a cup of hot water. "It's almost warm, pumpkin," she says to her small charge. He rests a paw no thicker than a straw on her arm and is soon sucking hungrily on a minuscule nipple.

# 39

# With Family Built In

### Jennifer Acosta and Her Family in Woodhaven, Queens

APRIL 11, 2010

Jennifer Acosta, an Ecuadorean immigrant, and her sons in a three-family house in Woodhaven, Queens. (Uli Seit for *The New York Times*)

F by some miracle you could slice off the front of Jennifer Acosta's red- and cream-colored house in Woodhaven, Queens, as if it were one of those dollhouses that open to reveal what lies within, you would find most of the people she feels closest to in the world.

Ms. Acosta, who's divorced and works in Manhattan as a personal assistant, shares the ground-floor unit with her son Derek, who is 12, and his 5-year-old brother, JanPaul. The second floor is home to her older sister, Jacqueline Andrade, who works as a nanny; Jacqueline's husband, Diego, who installs hardwood floors; and their 16-year-old daughter, Fernanda. On the top floor live Ms. Acosta's older brother, Luis Garcia, a warehouse supervisor, along with his wife, Alexandra, a former day-care worker, and their 14-year-old son, Calvin.

Even siblings besotted with one another might think twice about placing themselves under a single roof, especially one that looks barely large enough to shelter three households. But for these Ecuadorean immigrants, who were raised largely in a one-bedroom apartment near Fordham Road in the Bronx, the arrangement offered an escape from cramped quarters in a troubled part of the city.

Theirs is the contemporary immigrant story, one that involves shuttling between homeland and New York, husbands separated from wives, children separated from parents and attending schools both here and there, parents holding down typical immigrant jobs (the father was a cab driver), and everyone struggling to learn English as they inch closer to legal residence in the United States.

Ms. Acosta and her brother and sister had long talked about buying a place together. Yet only seven years ago, when they were shown this century-old house opposite Forest Park, did they realize they had found something both large enough to accommodate three separate households and priced at a level they could afford. "We'd been looking for a year," Ms. Acosta says. "The day we saw this house, we had already seen seven other places. This was the last one." The driveway shared with the house next door almost proved a deal breaker; initially, Ms. Andrade refused even to set foot inside the front door.

They bought the house for $400,000, dividing the down payment equally among the three families. The sharing continues, and in meticulous fashion. On the 15th of each month, Ms. Andrade takes a check for the mortgage to the bank. Mr. Garcia makes sure the taxes are paid. Ms.

Acosta administers to the sometimes temperamental boiler, a task she's proud that she mastered on her own.

A strict schedule spells out who's responsible for sorting the recyclables (Mr. Garcia in January, Ms. Andrade in February, Ms. Acosta in March, and so on). The three take turns shoveling snow and raking leaves. When it comes to tending the small front garden, a task that includes putting up Christmas decorations, everyone pitches in, kids included. Every summer, the three families buy something new—one year it was a fence, another a new front door. When something breaks, the cost of repairing it is divided into thirds. The arrangement sounds like something out of a 21st-century version of *The Brady Bunch*, this one set in a working-class immigrant neighborhood whose main drag, Jamaica Avenue, is lined with fluorescent-lit fast-food restaurants and shadowed by an el.

On occasion, one of those meticulously worked-out arrangements goes awry, memorably the time Ms. Andrade forgot to make the mortgage payment and her brother had to rush to the bank with a check minutes before the doors closed. And even people who love one another dearly can conclude that togetherness has its limits. "You know everyone's schedule," Ms. Acosta says. "You lack a certain privacy." A family member tiptoeing home late at night should expect pointed questions the next morning. "On the other hand," she says, "if there's a problem, like somebody's making too much noise, it's a lot easier to sort it out with a relative. And with the children, it's so much more secure not having strangers in the building."

Certain shared practices have assumed the quality of ritual. When Hilda Perez, the matriarch of the family, telephones from Ecuador, everyone converges on Ms. Andrade's apartment to talk to her on speakerphone. Because Calvin and Fernanda have back-to-back July birthdays, that occasion is always a big event. But really, any excuse will do. "We celebrate everything, and I mean everything," Ms. Acosta says.

In good weather, festivities take place in the concrete yard behind the house, generally on a Saturday night. Tables and chairs are dragged out, and everyone pitches in to grill pork ribs, chicken, and skirt steak. The adults play cards, and the loser gets dumped in the inflatable pool. On warm nights, the adults linger until 4 in the morning; the next day, there's ceviche on the menu to chase away hangovers.

Ms. Acosta, at 32 the baby of the family, has the smallest of the three units, the one with the lowest ceilings and the least light. Yet thanks to the generous use of mirrors and sunburst-bright colors, the spaces seem cheerful. In the living area, a mirrored wall that hides the washer and dryer doubles the apparent size of the room. Walls, rugs, and curtains are a medley of rust, tangerine, and pale pink, tones echoed by bottles of Zhumir, an Ecuadorean liquor, in flavors of mango, peach, and watermelon. Real flowers would never survive in these shadowy rooms, but artificial ones bloom everywhere.

The first year Ms. Acosta lived here, she was so broke from making the down payment, her only furnishings were castoffs from the apartment in the Bronx. But piece by piece, she gradually accumulated new stuff; she remembers how excited she was when she opened the boxes. And along with family memorabilia, among them a photograph of Derek suited up for his kindergarten graduation in a royal-blue cap and gown, her apartment is rich in religious artifacts. Derek serves as an altar boy at nearby Holy Child Jesus Church, and the room he and his brother share features ecclesiastical touches mixed in with the usual guy stuff. Along with Derek's Thomas the Tank Engine bedspread and the gold-colored belt he won for wrestling ("I was hoping they'd have a picture of their mother, but no," Ms. Acosta says), there are silvery crosses on the wall and, on a table, JanPaul's children's Bible with a rainbow on the cover.

The most beguiling religious display is the array of porcelain statues of the Virgin Mary in a corner cabinet in the living room. Some wear robes trimmed with gold rickrack, and every year Ms. Acosta sews new outfits for them. One statue, which Ms. Acosta has draped with wooden rosary beads, was found outside her old Bronx apartment. "I was standing on the street, and I just saw it there in the garbage," she says. "I could hear it calling me." She also has an assortment of baby Jesuses, five plastic infants that she brings out every Christmas and arranges in a Nativity scene.

The babies and the madonnas are charming, as are the sun-splashed furnishings, but Ms. Acosta's favorite item of décor is a small framed drawing in black crayon that hangs in the narrow hallway. "I tell people this is by a famous person," she says. In fact, the artist is Derek, and the praise makes him squirm. "You just say you like the drawing because I'm the one who made it," he complains. To which Ms. Acosta replies, "It's my apartment. I can do what I want."

# 40

# Threading the Needle on West 12th Street

Nancy Smith, John Casey, and Their Daughters in the West Village

APRIL 18, 2010

Nancy Smith, John Casey, and their daughters in their pre–Civil War town house in the West Village. (Librado Romero/*The New York Times*)

B ACK in the mid-1990s, when John Casey and Nancy Smith were about 30 and looking for an affordable place to live in the West Village, Mr. Casey chose an unusual approach to house hunting. Both he and his wife held midlevel jobs in publishing, and only by finding a distressed property that could generate income did they have a prayer of being able to afford what they wanted. So day after day, Mr. Casey prowled the narrow, tree-lined streets in search of rundown buildings. Then he pored over records at the offices of various city agencies, hoping to locate an owner who was financially on the ropes and thus desperate to sell.

"I started out going to the Surrogate's Court," Mr. Casey says. "When that proved completely useless, I began going to the City Registrar's office. I'd find addresses of owners and write them letters. I'd tell them we were a nice couple who wanted to own a house, and if they wanted to sell their house to us, we'd promise to take good care of it."

In 1997, after a hundred such letters, the couple struck gold. But they did so the old-fashioned way, through an ad they saw in the newspaper.

Gold might not seem the word to describe the red-brick town house on 12th Street in the West Village that had seen little love since its construction shortly before the Civil War. The four floors of what had started life as a single-family home had been mercilessly chopped into small apartments, and the structure was so run-down that Ms. Smith called it "the loser house on the block."

Despite the obvious drawbacks, Mr. Casey and Ms. Smith bought the building for $640,000 and discovered that the challenges associated with this particular address were just beginning. All six apartments were occupied, and all the tenants were protected by rent regulation, as a consequence of which dislodging any of them was likely be protracted and arduous.

At one point, the couple slept in the attic, a space that had neither heat nor electricity, not to mention ceilings so low that Mr. Casey, at 5-foot-11, could barely stand. "Our friends would come to visit us, and they'd be shocked," Ms. Smith says. "They'd say, 'We're very worried about you.'" But as one by one the tenants left, the couple colonized successive parts of the house. Today, except for two apartments on the second floor and one in the basement, they occupy the entire building, which today is also home to the couple's three daughters: Roma, 9, and Beatrice, 7, both adopted from China, and Frances, who is nearly 4.

The story might have ended differently had Mr. Casey not turned out to be an ace carpenter with a special touch when it came to historic details. The grandson of a pipe fitter whose Republic Steel helmet hangs on a wall in the kitchen, he's almost entirely self-taught, "or I should say *This Old House* taught." Yet despite the absence of formal training, Mr. Casey proved remarkably adept at nursing a troubled building back to health.

He removed collapsing ceilings. He stripped floors to reveal wide-plank hemlock and eastern white pine. He installed gas lines, built a laundry room ("and does all the laundry," his wife notes). He transformed a onetime kitchen into a bathroom, laying black and white tile on the floor and buying a shower online. "Somehow he not only figured out what we wanted, he also figured out how to do it," Ms. Smith says. Except for the kitchen and the attic, which were retrofitted with the help of an architect, he did nearly all the work himself, stripping 150 years of paint from intricate moldings and dragging tons of old plaster to Dumpsters in five-gallon buckets.

Mr. Casey's most impressive feat involved re-creating the long-absent front stoop, using period photographs from the building's early days to guide him. Working with a contractor, he rebuilt the concrete steps, then went online to order black wrought-iron railings from China. Even including shipping and customs duties, Mr. Casey paid only $700 for what he estimates might have cost $10,000 had he followed a more conventional route. And his measuring proved so meticulous and the drawings that he faxed to China so carefully executed that the railings received approval from the city's Landmarks Preservation Commission, required because the house is in a historic district.

Another story the couple tells involves the lighting fixture in the dining area, a white fiberglass sphere that resembles some ghostly planet come to rest in a quiet residential neighborhood. "I saw it on Craigslist at 2 in the morning," Ms. Smith says. "It had come from Design Within Reach and was originally $1,100, but they were asking just $300." Carless, her husband made his way to the Brooklyn neighborhood where the seller lived, then gingerly carted the fixture home on the subway, narrowly avoiding disaster when the doors snapped shut just inches from their new acquisition.

And speaking of Craigslist: the house could pose as an ad for the happy surprises to be found there, or perhaps in the "scratch and dent" section of Ikea, where the couple found a $400 dining table marked down to $99. Other items came from the Design Within Reach warehouse in Secaucus, New Jersey (Ms. Smith made friends with the manager), from neighbors (the white marble fireplace in a hallway), from flea markets (the turquoise china in the living room), from eBay (the Johnny Cash poster), even from an old boss of Ms. Smith's (the Japanese maple in the garden). "When people see this place," Ms. Smith says, "they think we have a lot of money. But the fact is, we bought nothing full price."

The presence of three little girls has added charm. A photo of the girls, each holding a brightly colored umbrella and looking as if they might fly up in the air, hangs opposite the fireplace in the parlor floor. The two older girls sleep in yellow bunk beds, and the parlor floor is carpeted with their toys, among them a wooden cradle that Ms. Smith's grandfather built for her when she was a child.

The mother of a preschool classmate of Frances's who's a frequent visitor says the house reminds her of houses in the Notting Hill neighborhood of London, "at least the movie version with Hugh Grant." She admires the open kitchen, the fireplace in the living room, the rear garden. She finds the spaces warm and airy. But behind the lovely details lie complicated lives. Both Mr. Casey and Ms. Smith have been buffeted by the recession, especially an unemployment rate that shows little signs of easing. Ms. Smith was laid off last October from her job as the creative director at the Parenting Group, and her husband, who held various magazine jobs, has been a stay-at-home parent for eight years. Both are trying to reinvent themselves to cope with hard times. Ms. Smith recently started a consulting business called I Know Moms, aimed at the parenting market. Mr. Casey hopes to find a wider audience for his carpentry skills via a Web site called Handydadsnyc.

The couple's lives have been complicated in other respects. Before Frances was born, they were told they would never be able to have a biological child. Mr. Casey has written candidly about his struggles with alcoholism and depression and his fears that genes for both conditions would be passed to a future generation.

Nor, despite the pristine look of their home today, did the look come easily. Given the dismal state of the house when they bought it and the number of entrenched tenants, there was considerable risk involved. And all the do-it-yourself carpentry and middle-of-the-night purchases on Craigslist speak to the challenges of making do during economic hard times.

Over the years the couple spent $200,000 in renovations, and this isn't to mention the psychic costs of nursing an ailing building back to life. "We have friends who say, 'We've never known you when your house wasn't being torn up,'" Ms. Smith says. "And even though we did a lot of things right, we did a lot of things wrong." Case in point: the bricks were pointed twice—first badly, then properly. She's also quick to acknowledge that her husband—Casey, as she calls him—did the bulk of the work. "I spent a couple of weekends stripping royal-blue paint from the hallway, and that was it," Ms. Smith says. "It was really Casey's sweat and blood that made this happen. He really threaded the needle."

# About the Author

Constance Rosenblum, who wrote the Habitats column published in the Real Estate section of *The New York Times*, is the longtime editor of the paper's City section and a former editor of *The Times*'s Arts and Leisure section. She is the author of *Boulevard of Dreams: Heady Times, Heartbreak, and Hope along the Grand Concourse in the Bronx*.